Spy Fever: The Post Office Affair

Spy Fever
The Post Office Affair

Margaret Flaws

The Shetland Times Ltd.
2009

Spy Fever: The Post Office Affair

First published by The Shetland Times Ltd., 2009

Copyright © Margaret Flaws, 2009

ISBN: 987-1-904746-38-6

Printed and published by
The Shetland Times Ltd.,
Gremista, Lerwick,
Shetland ZE1 0PX.

for Ian

Contents

AS A BOY growing up in Lerwick in the 1920s and 1930s, the son of one of the imprisoned Post Office staff, I had some slight knowledge of that event which took place some seven years before my birth. On the rare occasions that my father did mention it he spoke mostly of how he and other junior members of the staff made the best they could of this unexpected respite from the long working hours they had been obliged to undertake since the war started. Twenty of them, my father included, were aged under thirty and, as he later wrote: "We all had a clear conscience and feared no one, so why worry?"

They enjoyed the camaraderie and the opportunity to relax with their colleagues, although my father must have resented being parted from his wife after two months of marriage. The presentation of a wedding gift from his colleagues, within the local prison, must surely be unique. Had the staff known that the Post Office would later consider withholding their wages for the week spent in prison (on the grounds that they didn't report for duty) I don't think any of them would have felt relaxed about their situation.

George Manson with John H Manson and grandson Paul at the Knab in Lerwick in July 1961.

Photo: Courtesy of John H Manson

It was in 1955, seven years after his retirement from the Post Office, and forty-one years after the event, that my father was persuaded by a friend to commit to paper his recollections of the arrest and incarceration. A copy of his story reached the BBC offices in Glasgow and formed the basis of a radio play titled *To Prison on Sunday*, broadcast on 29th February 1957. No new information was then available to solve the mystery behind the arrest, or release without any explanation, but the radio broadcast did emphasise the 'enemy spy fever' which was apparently widespread throughout the nation in the early months of the First World War.

By painstaking research, and with the aid of modern information technology, Margaret Flaws has pieced together a mass of relevant information from government archives. The results of her research expose some salient aspects of the arrest and its aftermath:

1. The primary reason for the drastic action taken to arrest the Lerwick Post Office staff would appear to stem from the unfounded, but deep-rooted, doubts about the loyalty of Shetlanders held by the Admiralty, including the First Lord, Winston Churchill.
2. The officer commanding the troops in Shetland was, to put it mildly, inept in his handling of the affair and, apparently, ignorant of the vital role played by the Lerwick Post Office as a link in the international telegraph network.
3. Officialdom in London, including the Postmaster General and his staff, adopted a detached attitude towards the whole affair, as being far away and of little concern. The transfer from Lerwick of the highly-respected postmaster, who led the quest for justice, was a deliberate ploy in the hope that removing the 'Chief' would discourage the 'natives' from pursuing the matter.

Margaret Flaws is to be congratulated for revealing much of what went on behind the scenes in this unprecedented affair. It would be comforting to say that now, almost a century later, such a travesty of justice could not happen in the UK … or could it?

John H Manson

Acknowledgements

I AM INDEBTED to many people for help and information. Some of these were relatives of those thrown in jail; Mrs Robina Martin (nee Mackay) whose father was jailed; Mrs C Fraser whose uncle was J Thomson; Jim Mustard, a nephew of Jimmy Williamson and Bob Williamson.

Among others who helped are Mr James Wishart, Mr Douglas Twitchen, James Miller, author of the North Atlantic Front, Alistair Carmichael MP and his secretary, Diane Davidson, the staff at Heritage Royal Mail and the Scottish National Archives, Tim Hughes for research at the National Archives at Kew, and Brian Smith and staff at Shetland Museum and Archives.

I owe special thanks to John Fergusson for letting me read his grandfather's diary and allowing me to use material from it.

This book, however, could not have been written without the help and support and encouragement of John Manson. He has allowed me to use his father's articles and letters written to him by Jimmy Williamson and Postmaster Macmaster. He has also read and corrected each chapter as it was written. So thank you, John. Here is your book.

Introduction

THIS IS A story I grew up with. It was part of the fabric of family life, embedded in the family history and it was only gradually that I realised that it was not just our family that it belonged to; other people's grandfathers had been thrown in jail on the same day. Members of other families had been accused of being spies. My grandfather was not unique.

I heard the story from my mother, Jean, who grew up in Lerwick and who was eleven when these events took place. She remembered them clearly. My grandfather never spoke about it. My mother told me that she and her sisters used to tease my grandfather about being a jailbird but he could not share their laughter. He could never be brought to see anything funny in it at all. It was a measure of how serious he considered the situation was at the time.

As time passed more information was added to the story. I discovered the articles written by George Manson, who had been jailed along with my grandfather and the thin thread of the family story expanded into cloth. Here were all the familiar details with a wealth of other information. It was fascinating. My grandfather in jail for spying was no longer an exciting tale to equal *The Famous Five*. It was real; it had happened. I wanted to know more. But other things took precedence for some time.

At length I realised that I had better write down the family story as I had heard it because there were some details in that which were not mentioned in other accounts. This was the catalyst which led me into the search that has resulted in this book.

The Shetland Archives were a great source of information. Not only did they have George Manson's excellent articles, they also had a number of relevant newspaper cuttings. Those in turn led to a trawl through *The Scotsman* archives on the internet and I found still more there. A hunt through the archives of the Orkney papers in the library in Kirkwall provided some more accounts of the event, but all of these were merely newspaper accounts. They told of the arrest but could give no reasons for it. They had not been told the reason for the arrest. Nobody had been told the reason for the arrest, least of all those arrested. I thought there must be more information somewhere and began to search.

J J (Hug) Tait on holiday after he retired. The picture was taken in Lerwick around 1949/1950 with his daughter Jean Arthur (left) and sister-in-law Martha Brown (nee Leask).

To begin with, I was not sure if I would find anything at all. After all, it was a long time ago; it was in what people from the mainland of Britain call a 'remote part of the country', without realising of course that, to us, a remote part of the country is Edinburgh or London. It was probably, in the great scheme of World War 1, regarded as a minor incident. I started my search, therefore, with no very high hopes. I was to be proved wrong.

My own home is in Orkney on an island, a small island. There are eighteen of us living here and that includes my three grandchildren. We do not consider ourselves remote at all, but living here does present some problems when it comes to doing research. It must be done by post or by the internet.

Most of mine was done by post, which seems appropriate in the circumstances. I can glance out of my window and watch the ferry bringing the mail across. We have a tiny Post Office here and I can see this from my window too and I can watch Heather coming up the road with her mailbag. Thus my information began to arrive, first in a trickle, then in a flood.

I wrote first to the Head Post Office in Edinburgh asking if they had any lists of staff in Lerwick in 1914. I explained that I was interested in the arrest of November 1914 and hoped rather than expected that they could supply some names. A reply came from Heritage Royal Mail in London saying that my letter had been passed on to them, they had looked up the file and there were several relevant documents. I could have copies of these for a small fee. This was exciting. When the documents arrived, delivered by Heather, I tried not to expect too much but I need not have worried. There was a mass of information in them.

My chief correspondent at that time on this subject was George Manson's son, John, who had also written several articles on the subject. I copied the information I had received from the Post Office to send to him. He was as astonished as I was that so many relevant papers had been preserved. He was also incensed at the content of some of them. It seemed that there was much more to the story than either of us had believed. And then I read a curious statement in a book by James Miller, *The North Atlantic Front.* He mentioned the Lerwick Post Office arrest as perhaps being the result of an opinion at the Admiralty at that time that there was reason to doubt the loyalty of the Shetlanders. He cited as his evidence for this an Admiralty paper in the National Archives at Kew.

The National Archives are online but a search on the internet provided the numbers and references of papers only. To read these papers and follow up the clues in them would mean a visit to London and that was not possible. Again the Post Office came to my rescue. They had sent me a list of agents who would undertake research for a fee and I picked one from their list. Once more I was lucky. The research agent I found, Tim Hughes, was very efficient. He found two relevant papers and I was stunned when I read them. Doubts of the loyalty of the Shetlanders had been expressed at the highest level, at a meeting chaired by Prime Minister Asquith, and they had been voiced by the First Lord of the Admiralty, Winston Churchill. I found it difficult to believe and asked Tim to check for other references but he could find none.

I hunted on the internet once more to see if there might be another source of information on this and found a curious reference in *The Churchill Papers.* At one point, 31st October, 1911, Churchill sent a minute to the Director of Naval Intelligence Rear-Admiral Alexander Bethell asking, among other things, about German influence in the Shetland Islands. Bethell replied that German influence was not very marked in the islands and that no German ships had been there since 1904. He included a report on the number and distribution of the population and a list of ships that had visited Shetland since 1909. This reference made it all the more strange that Churchill should insist, in the meeting in the following year, that the loyalty of the Shetlanders was suspect.

I approached the MP for Orkney and Shetland, Alistair Carmichael, for help in finding any references in *Hansard* and it was his secretary who suggested I should try the Scottish National Archives. I wrote to them. Apparently they had documents also. I applied for copies and struck gold. Here were all the Prison Commission papers, letters, reports and a copy of the Prison Register for 1st November, 1914. My grandfather's name was second on the list, after the Postmaster. I read his name, his age, his address and I wept. It was no longer just a family story. It had turned into a tragedy. Till that moment I had found it difficult to believe that my beloved grandfather could ever have been thrown into jail. Here was proof incontrovertible.

The search for information had come to an end. There were no more sources of papers to try. Now what had been just a vague idea of recording a family story had evolved, for me, into a kind of crusade. I wanted the explanation and apology from the authorities that my grandfather had never achieved. Failing that, I wanted to record the circumstances of the arrest and the reasons, however feeble, that had surfaced. I began to write.

In the midst of writing and rewriting, a strange coincidence occurred. In our local paper, *The Orcadian,* I read an article by John Fergusson about his grandfather's diary, which he had kept in the first years of World War 1. Almost leaping off the page was a reference to doubts about the loyalty of the Shetlanders. The last piece of the jigsaw slotted into place.

CHAPTER 1

1904, Lerwick, Shetland

APRIL – Lerwick in 1904 was a thriving, busy, growing town. In the herring season it was full of bustle and noise; hammering from the coopers' yards, the clatter of wooden clogs on the cobbles, the babble of different languages.

Along Commercial Street the pervasive smell of fish mingled with sudden drifts of cologne from handkerchiefs generously soaked from bottles carried by the Dutch fishermen. At times the harbour became choked with fishing boats till it seemed it might be possible to walk dry shod from Lerwick to Bressay. Local businesses thrived and people grew in confidence.

On the evening of Wednesday, 27th April, the newly-formed Lerwick Amateur Orchestral Society gave a performance. It was billed as a classical concert and was hailed a great triumph. The orchestra had asked Thomas Manson to be their conductor and he had led them successfully through some lighter pieces to a difficult work by Handel. The instrumentalists had come together through their love of music and it was inevitable that, in a small town like Lerwick, many of them were also colleagues at work or members of other groups.

James Tait, for example, who played the double bass, was a member of the Post Office staff, as was violinist Bob Mackay. They were also both members of the local Territorial Force. The people of Lerwick were linked in many ways, family, friends, colleagues, employers, employees. Everyone knew everyone else.

At the orchestra's next meeting they pronounced themselves well satisfied with their first public performance and vowed to work towards another.

JULY – Early on the morning of Saturday, 23rd July, at about five o'clock, two tenders and torpedo boats of the German Active Fleet made their way into the harbour at

Lerwick String Band in 1904. Back: Hug Tait, William Nicolson, William Harrison, Christie Gilbertson (leader), Thomas Manson (conductor), Dr Willcock (patron), Bob Mackay, Andrew J Abernethy. Middle: Louisa Leisk, Dotty Sandison, Hattie Leisk, Beatrice Hunter, V.Alger. Front: Magnus Anderson, Gideon Stove, A Murray.

Photo: A Abernethy. Shetland Museum and Archives Photo Library

The German Fleet at anchor in Lerwick in July 1904. Left (from front): SMS Kaiser Wilhelm II, SMS Kaiser Wilhelm der Grosse, SMS Kaiser Karl der Grosse, SMS Kaiser Friedrich III. Right (from front) SMS Mecklenburg, SMS Zahringen, SMS Wettin, SMS Wittelbach. The vessel in the front is one of 10 torpedo boats in the visiting fleet.

Photo: J D Ratter, Shetland Museum and Archives Photo Library

Lerwick. The coaling steamer *Hermann Sauber* had arrived two days earlier and lay awaiting the ships, ready to refuel them, and soon the torpedo boats were flocking round her like hungry gulls. There were few people about at this time but the crowd gradually increased, watching the busy scene in the harbour.

The dispatch ships *Blitz* and *Pfeil* came to the harbour entrance and took on board two local pilots, Robert Christie and Peter Hunter. At about eight o'clock they transferred to a torpedo boat which made its way out of the south entrance, heading southeast to meet the rest of the fleet. Once clear of the harbour it picked up speed, reaching 26 knots and cutting through the water like a knife, a green wave following in its wake.

It was after noon before a black mass of smoke on the horizon to the south heralded the arrival of the fleet and soon crowds gathered at the Knab, watching the ships approach, line behind line. In single file they steamed towards Lerwick, one after the other, until all thirty-two ships had anchored, some inside the harbour itself and the rest clustered round the Knab close by.

Derricks rattled and steam launches were lowered from the vessels and began plying back and fore. Sunshine lit the scene and lightened the grey on the towering ships. Those watching were invited to visit the ships and many did so, making their way out by steam launch and gazing at the awe-inspiring equipment on board. The crews were friendly and helpful, showing people all over the ships. When offered a tip one crewman refused, saying it was beneath the dignity of the German Fleet to accept.

At night the harbour seemed magical with the all-electric lights from the ships reflecting on the still water, the flashing signals, the red and green of the navigation lights on the steam launches and the Bressay light shining majestically over all.

During the three days that the fleet lay at Lerwick a carnival spirit spread over the town. Bands played on the ships all day. The crews came ashore late on Saturday, about 2,000 of them, and the shops stayed open for them. The crewmen bought postcards. The officers bought Shetland goods.

On Sunday 3,000 came ashore and wandered in and around Lerwick. Some ventured as far as Scalloway, walking all the way and singing lively marching songs. Their behaviour was exemplary and a credit to the German navy.

Sheriff Alexander Moffat and the German Vice-consul at Lerwick, Andrew John Robertson, paid an official visit on board and the vice-consul was honoured by a salute of five guns. After a formal return visit by the German admiral, von Koester, Sheriff Moffat and Mr Robertson were invited to dine on board the flagship *Kaiser Wilhelm II*.

On Monday the ships were provisioned and stores were bought locally by contract. The stewards, however, came ashore and went from shop to shop buying

3

extra goods. On Monday afternoon the battleships and cruisers put to sea and during the night fought a sham battle. The citizens of Lerwick had their sleep disturbed by the bangs of the guns.[1]

On Tuesday the fleet left for Norway.

At this time James J Tait was a telegraphist in the Lerwick Post Office. He had joined the Post Office at twelve years of age, which was quite young. Ordinarily he would have had to stay at school until he was fourteen but he had completed all the necessary work and passed all the necessary examinations by the time he was twelve so there seemed little point in remaining at school when he could be earning and helping the family. He had even managed to master some Latin declensions by that stage and would have liked to pursue this. He had a flair for languages and enjoyed learning.

By July, 1904, he was married, to Leebie Leask, and baby Jean was nine months old. They were living in Stove's Buildings, near the Hillhead, and Leebie's mother and two sisters lived with them along with Johnny, baby son of Leebie's sister Jessie. It was a crowded household.

Jessie was one of the few to see the arrival of the first of the fleet. She worked in the lemonade factory, the 'fizzy factory' as it was known locally, and she started work at five o'clock. She watched the tenders and the torpedo boats come in and during the morning looked out now and again to see what was happening.

By the time her sister, Mattie, arrived at the wool shop where she worked the harbour was busy. She had walked down the lane with her brother-in-law. He turned right to go to his shift at the Post Office and during the morning watched the scene as it unfolded whenever he could spare a moment. One of the telegraphists working with him, nineteen-year-old George Manson, kept slipping out to see what was happening and he kept them abreast of developments.

After work finished for the day James, known as Hug to his friends, walked along to the pier and went on board one of the launches taking people out to visit the ships. He noticed that George had managed to get ahead of him and was already on board. "Trust him!" he thought. Hug was impressed with the tidiness and efficiency of the launches, the towering height of the battleship and the friendliness of the crew. It was worth being late home for supper and he knew that he would be plied with questions when he did arrive home.

---

1   Visit of German Fleet – The Shetland Times, 30th July, 1904.

On Sunday, after church service, Hug, Leebie and Mattie took a walk around the Knab to look at the harbour, full to bursting with battleships and cruisers. There were many others watching the ships and still the feeling of excitement prevailed. Hug, however, felt uneasy and the sparkling scene in front of him began to assume an air of menace. He wondered why so many German ships had come there and did not like the answer that presented itself to him.

Back at work on Monday at the Post Office, Hug heard snatches of conversation among the staff and found that others in Lerwick had shared his sense of unease. Underneath the general air of excitement, which the visit of the ships had brought, there was a growing puzzlement regarding the real reason for such a visit. Many of the staff had seen the interest shown by the crews who came ashore in the harbour buildings, in the layout of the streets, even in the defences of Lerwick itself.

"Did you hear about Crocker at the fort?" someone asked. Officer Crocker RN was in charge of Fort Charlotte. He had said more than once that he did not trust the Germans and did not believe they had peaceful intentions.

"What about him?" said another.

"Some Germans asked if they could see round the fort. He wouldn't let them. He buckled on his sword and closed the gates and told them to go away in no uncertain terms."

"He could be right, at that."

"You know, they seemed to know the place pretty well, when you come to think of it. Some of the boats came in and out of the north entrance as cool as you please without a pilot!"

"I feel it's high time that our own fleet were showing an interest in us. The Germans maybe think that they don't care about us."

In July 1904 Captain Horace Carlyon Evans was in the Mediterranean. He was a captain in the Royal Marine Light Infantry and had transferred in April from HMS *Russell* to HMS *Queen*. Capt Evans was born in Ihansi in the North West Territory in India. His father was then a colonel in the Indian Service Corps. After spending some of his childhood in India, Horace Evans was first commissioned in the RMLI in September 1886 when he was twenty.

His service reports were invariably favourable until as a lieutenant he was sent to the Army Service Corps on probation. For whatever reason, his commanding officer at Aldershot found his conduct unsatisfactory and he was sent back to Chatham in 1892. In 1896 he was promoted to captain and the following year he was sent to

Manchester as adjutant to the 4th Volunteer Battalion of the Manchester Light Infantry. He served there to such good effect that they were unwilling to part with him when he was transferred in 1902.

After two years' service in the Mediterranean he was expecting, in July 1904, to be promoted to major and a month later his promotion came through.

On 30th July Hug Tait sat, in the evening after work, reading *The Shetland Times*. He found the account of the visit of the German Fleet the week before and folded the paper to look at it. It was a good, well-written article but it was the last paragraph that held his interest. In it there was a list of the visits of warships to Lerwick over the years.

"Listen to this," he said to Leebie. "It says here that there were two visits of English warships – lots of them by the look of it – in 1653 and 1665. Then nothing for 200 years until 1854 when the British White Fleet – only three of them – were here; 1861, seven of the Channel Fleet; 1883, English Reserve Squadron, nine of them. And since then, no sign of the British lot. Instead we've had two visits from the Germans. There were nine of them in 1900. I remember that. And now we've had thirty-two. Wonder if there will be any sign of the British in the near future."

"You would think they would pay a visit now and again," said Leebie. "There are enough Shetlanders in the navy to show them how to get here, surely."

SEPTEMBER – It had been more than twenty years since any British warship had been seen in Shetland waters, but in September the majority of the ships of the Channel Fleet were to pay a visit to Lerwick. On the seventeenth *The Shetland Times* carried an extensive account of the ships that were to arrive that very afternoon, with a list of the captains of each of them, a survey of the entertainments that had been prepared for them and a picture of the admiral in command with details of his career.

Included in the paper was a photograph of the new Volunteer Drill Hall, which Vice-Admiral Lord Charles Beresford was to open. He was to be escorted through the town to the drill hall by a contingent of the local Territorial Force, the Shetland Companies of Gordon Highlanders. At the hall the Admiral would be met by the other members of the battalion, under the command of Lieutenant Alexander Stephen. Volunteers from Orkney were coming north on the *St Rognvald* to be there also. In the evening the officers of the local battalion were to entertain the Admiral and a number of his officers in the Queen's Hotel.

The British Channel Fleet in Lerwick in 1904: HMS Mars, *HMS* Illustrious *and HMS* Caesar.

Photo: J D Rattar, Shetland Museum and Archives Photo Library

Crowds of people at the laying of the foundation stone of the Lerwick Drill Hall, now the Garrison Theatre.

Photo: Shetland Museum and Archives Photo Library

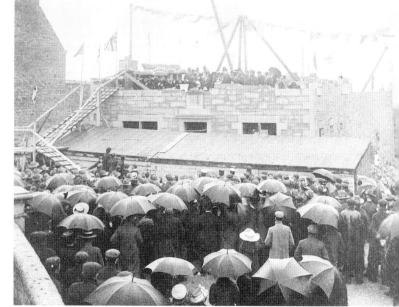

7

It promised to be an eventful day surpassed only by the entertainments arranged for the following Monday. There was to be a grand ball for the officers hosted by the county council and Lerwick Town Council. It was expected to be a huge gathering. The crews were not forgotten either. Two smoking concerts were to be held for them, with refreshments, in the drill hall and Fort Charlotte. The committee in charge of hospitality had arranged also for all of the available halls in Lerwick to be open while the fleet was in harbour and for tea and meals to be served there free for all the visitors.

The Shetland Times account was as lavish as the promised entertainment itself. The only discordant note among the fulsome prose was struck by the editorial. This pointed out the length of time that Shetland had had to wait for this visit but, on a theme of 'better late than never', said that the welcome might be all the warmer for it.[2]

The members of the Territorial Force polished their boots and smartened up their uniforms and made their way to the drill hall next to Fort Charlotte. The Shetland Volunteers had been reformed in 1900, with War Office permission. Originally the Volunteers had been part of the 1st Sutherland Rifles but when they were reformed they were attached to the Gordon Highlanders. This may have been in part because of the fact that Shetland contact with the Scottish Mainland had traditionally been through Aberdeen, but there is no doubt that agreement on this was only reached after a struggle. The fact that Lt Stephen came from Aberdeen perhaps had some bearing on the outcome also.

Hug Tait was a member of the Territorial Force. He had the afternoon off work to attend the opening and he made his way along the Hillhead, past the Town Hall and down to the drill hall. He found Lt Stephen there explaining to his contingent of volunteers the order of the day. They settled down to await the arrival of the Admiral.

The Lerwick people read their papers and awaited the arrival of the ships. Many strolled down to the harbour to watch for them coming. Fifteen ships were said to be coming and although this was less than half of the number of splendid German ships that they had seen earlier in the year, it was yet a good number and it showed that the British Navy recognised and valued Shetland and the Shetlanders. Considering the number of Shetlanders, then and in the past, who had served in the Royal Navy, this was only to be expected. Still, it was fine to be appreciated.

A rumour spread through the crowd that eleven ships only were to arrive. More people arrived to watch and they were soon joined by shop workers as the shops in

2   Visit of British Fleet – The Shetland Times – 17th September, 1904.

Lerwick were to be closed between three and five in the afternoon so that everyone had the chance to see the ceremony.

Soon there was a stirring among the crowd as the first ship rounded the Knab and approached the harbour. It was followed by another and another and another. And that was that. Four ships steamed into the harbour and the crowd looked in vain for more.

As the Admiral got into his launch to come ashore, a voice in the crowd was heard to mutter: "Four ships? Is that all?" They watched in silence as the Admiral reached the pier, climbed into one of the waiting carriages and, accompanied by local dignitaries, set off for the drill hall.

When Hug Tait came home, after the drill hall had been well and truly opened, he found Leebie and Mattie talking, in disgusted tones, about the day's events.

"Only four boats!" said Leebie. "Only four and the Germans sent thirty-two!"

"Looks as though the Germans think more of us than our own Navy does, for all the Shetland men that are in it!"

"How did the opening go?" asked Leebie.

"Fine," said Hug. "Lots of speeches, as you would expect."

"Interesting?"

"Well, the Provost said that he thought the Admiral would know Lerwick Harbour better than we did ourselves. Which I thought was a bit silly."

"Only a bit?" said Mattie. "The man's never been here."

"What was the Admiral like?" asked Leebie.

"Oh! All right I suppose," said Hug. "At least Lieutenant Stephen was made up to captain because of his visit, which is something."

"Did he say why there were only four boats instead of the whole fleet?"

"All he really said was that wherever the Admiral was, that was the Fleet."

"Well," said Mattie. "He can't be much of an Admiral with a peerie fleet of four boats. He could sail that in his bath!"

Predictably, in the following Saturday's paper, the editor of *The Shetland Times* had a field day.[3] The anger and resentment of the people of Lerwick at the perceived insult of being worth only four ships of His Britannic Majesty's Navy had been rumbling away all week, building up pressure, which was released in a blast of laughter as the townspeople read the editorial.

---

3   Editorial *The Shetland Times* – 24th September, 1904.

"Listen to this," said Hug. "The Phantom Fleet, he calls it!"

"I told you," said Mattie. "He could have put it in his bath."

"I heard," said Leebie, "that the council were a bit upset after all the entertainment that they had laid on. The officers at the ball were few and far between."

"What else does he say?" asked Mattie.

"He's talking about the harbour," said Hug, reading rapidly. "He says that the navy is making the same old excuse that the harbour is inadequate, when it's one of the finest natural harbours in the kingdom." He burst out laughing.

"What's funny in that?" asked Leebie.

"He says that Provost Leisk's remarks – remember I told you about that? – must have sounded like unconscious sarcasm, and – wait for this – he says that if the navy want a little better information about the harbour 'a polite request might be addressed to the German authorities.'" Hug's eyes twinkled and his faced creased in laughter.

"Well! Did you ever!" said Leebie.

"They deserved that," said Mattie.

A few days after the Shetlanders had laughed their way through the editorial, a clerk in the Admiralty in London was reading it thoughtfully. Some time later he was instructed to file it carefully.

In October 1904 Maj Evans was relieved of his appointment on HMS *Queen* and ordered to return overland from Trieste to England where he took up duties on shore at Plymouth Division and was to remain there until the next year.

1907

BY 1907 Hug Tait had moved his family from Stove's Buildings to Havelock Cottage. Leebie's mother and two sisters were still living with them and the tiny cottage seemed quite cramped at times. Jean was now three-and-a-half and her little sister, Mary, was almost two. Jean called her 'baby sissie' and the name stayed with her. After that she was just known as Cissie. Havelock Cottage was just down the lane from the Town Hall and a stone's throw from Lerwick Prison.

By now also the Post Office telegraph department had become extremely busy. The Great Northern Telegraph Co. had laid a cable from Burwick in Shetland to Torshavn in Faroe and then to Iceland. They had made an agreement with the Post Office to carry their signals and the Lerwick Post Office now carried all the traffic from Denmark to its dependent territories in the Faeroes and Iceland. Hug had begun to learn Danish in order to ensure accuracy in transmission. He was adept at sending and receiving telegraph signals.

Telegraphists were being trained as quickly as possible but it took time. Once trained, they were in great demand and a few had left the Lerwick office for other stations in Shetland. As well as the Danish traffic, there were numerous cables for local businesses. It was the only quick means of communicating with the rest of Britain. Added to that were the demands of the fishing industry. In the height of the season it was often possible to walk dry shod across the harbour from deck to deck of the massed boats. It was by no means unheard of for telegraph staff to be recalled after their shifts to work through another accumulation of cables.

One of those training to become a telegraphist was Jimmy Williamson. In 1907 he was fifteen. His father was a baker and the family lived in Mounthooly Street. Jimmy had joined the Post Office in the usual manner, as a telegram boy, and was now looking forward to a full-time career. He had a lively sense of humour and was popular with the staff. He meant to join the Territorial Force when he was old enough as he thought it would be interesting. He would get some training with guns perhaps.

George Manson had left the Lerwick Post Office in 1904 and gone to work in the sub-post office at Tresta as a telegraphist. He had family connections with the place and had a great fondness for it, but by 1907 he was restless, looking for adventure and a new path to tread. He was 22. He had read a lot about Australia and thought that perhaps there he could find a new opportunity in life.[1] He decided to emigrate.

He left Lerwick on the *St Rognvald*, bound for Leith. From Edinburgh he took the train to Newcastle where his brother John was living and from there he left, on Thursday 18th April, on the midnight train to London. It was his first trip away from home.

On the same train was an Australian, of Scottish descent, who had served an apprenticeship in engineering in Scotland and was returning to Australia. Together they travelled to London and on to Tilbury to board the ship. George listened carefully to all that his friend could tell him. Everything around him was new and exciting. Each day brought fresh images crowding into his mind.

Through the Mediterranean they went, from Gibraltar to Marseilles and on to Naples where the sun shone on little white houses and sparkling blue sea. George gazed at Vesuvius, rising straight up, cone-shaped, with its chimney of smoke.

When they entered the Suez Canal, they marvelled at how narrow it was, how they had to lean over the side of the ship to catch a glimpse of the water. "What if we meet a ship coming the other way?" asked George. His Australian companion had travelled this way before and could tell him that there were passing places. "There are notices there," he said " 'Gare limite nord', and 'Gare limite sud'. In between you can pass."

The air got hotter and hotter. George thought it felt as though it came straight from Hell. At Suez the ship stopped to land the pilot and then steamed off at full speed down the Gulf of Suez. Far from bringing a welcome breeze to cool them, it grew hotter still and the pitch between the deck planks became soft and bubbly. Below deck at dinner the heat was almost unbearable. George turned to his friend and remarked: "My soup is getting watered down. The sweat is dropping off my nose onto my plate."

---

1   Events in George Manson's life from his article "Impressions of Distant Lands".

George Manson in 1913.

Photo: Courtesy of Lerwick Post Office

That evening, George was intrigued by the sight of some of the crew carrying a large roll of canvas aft. He watched intently as they began to unroll it. "What is this you're working at?" he asked. "This," said a crewman, "is a tank for you to swim in during the hot weather. We will have it ready and pumped full of water tomorrow morning."

That night was the first of many that George chose to sleep on deck. Some others joined him. They were woken at 4.30 am by crewmen coming to wash down the decks and had to take their mattresses below. However, to compensate, the tank was full by 5 am and George lost no time in diving in.

From the seventh of May to the thirteenth they sailed through calm blue glittering seas to Colombo. From time to time shoals of flying fish – like flocks of little white birds – emerged with a splash and a whirr, dropping one by one into the water again and leaving only a few ripples which presently subsided.

After taking on a cargo of tea, the ship left its last port of call before landfall in Australia and headed south. George was looking forward to crossing the equator. It would be quite an event to leave his own world in the north and reach the southern hemisphere. It would also be very hot indeed, he thought. It was meant to be the hottest part of the earth.

They sailed, however, from hot blue skies into damp and misty weather and soon the rain fell in torrents on the ship's deck. George complained to one of the crew who told him that the weather was generally dull and damp in that latitude. "Sailing ships can lie here becalmed for weeks sometimes. This bit is known as the Doldrums."

Finally, on 23rd May the ship arrived at Freemantle. Many of the passengers left there but George travelled on to Sydney and sailed into the impressive harbour, wondering at all he saw.

George stayed for a time in Sydney considering what he should do in this vast new country. It was never difficult for him to make friends and he made many new friends there. One, in particular, he found good company and they spent a lot of time together. He was a young aboriginal who had been brought up by Scots people. The man had found him lying all alone on a hillside when he was about eighteen months old and he took him home to his wife. He joined their family and went to school with their children. He proved an apt pupil and when he had finished school he got a post as a draughtsman. He was twenty-one when George met him.

As Scots had brought him up, he spoke Scots. He also at times wore Highland dress and played the bagpipes.

One evening when George met him there was a broad grin on his face. "What are you laughing at?" asked George.

"You'll never believe this. This morning an engineer off one of the 'home' boats came into the office. He came from Glasgow and he spoke broad Scots. So for a joke I did the same, and you should have seen his face! Then the boss came in and I went back to my desk. They went out of the room but I heard him say to the boss, 'Guid Lord, man, whar did ye get that black Scotsman frae?'" George burst out laughing. "I'll remember that!" he said.

The newspapers in Sydney were full of glowing accounts of the land that could be had further north and the living that could be earned from it. George went to the government land office and got a job on the land at a place called Raleigh, about 300 miles north of Sydney. He wanted to see as much of the country as he could. He thought perhaps this would be the best way forward for him. It took him five days to make the journey by boat and on foot.

He found that, although it was true that land could be purchased very cheaply, it cost a great deal to clear and to cultivate, and to build a homestead on it. He found also that because of the costs and the meagre returns most farmers worked away from home and the women ran the farm. He thought it was much like the system of crofting in Shetland. It was not the Utopia he had crossed the world to find.

Disillusioned, he returned to Sydney and decided to sign on as crew. He shipped on board a barque bound for New Zealand and left Australia.

In 1907, Maj Evans was serving in the Mediterranean on HMS *Venerable*. In the previous year he had submitted a series of reports on the defence of Lisbon. For this work he had received an expression of their Lordships' appreciation. He was now engaged in the gathering of intelligence on the Greek Navy and the docks at Piraeus. He duly submitted this report and once again received an expression of their Lordships' appreciation.

In August that year he transferred to HMS *Prince of Wales* and remained there until the spring of the following year when he was posted to HMS *Tamar*, the shore station in Hong Kong. He was to continue in his involvement with intelligence, gathering information on Chinese forts.

CHAPTER 3

1910

HUG TAIT had moved his family from Havelock Cottage. After his third daughter, Leebie, was born in 1908 the house began to seem cramped, bursting at the seams. Grandmother Jean had a little room to herself and Mattie and Jessie shared the other bedroom with Johnny. This left the main room downstairs for Hug and Leebie and their three daughters.

They looked for somewhere with a bit more space and found a home at 12 Commercial Street. It seemed a mansion after the cottage and even had a flush toilet on the ground floor. Everyone settled in happily and in June another daughter arrived to swell the family.

"What do we call this one?" asked Hug. A boy would have been nice for a change, he thought, but Leebie and the baby were fine and that was all that mattered.

"Well," said Leebie. "Jean was called after my mother. Cissie was called after your mother. Leebie is named for me, so this one will be named for you, I think. You're James John so she should be Jemima Joan."

"Oh, no," groaned Hug. "You can have the one or the other but not both!"

"But the others have two names each," protested Leebie.

"I don't care. One will be enough. You cannot call the poor lass Jemima Joan."

So she was called Joan; blonde-haired, chubby Joan. Nobody called her Joan. She was Joey.

Jean and Johnny loved the new house. It was right at the water's edge, battered by the sea in the winter, a perch for herring gulls. There was a cellar under the house with a yard behind it, a cooper's yard. In the cellar barrels were made for the herring fishing and in the season it was busy and noisy. Under the cellar there was a lodberry, another cellar with access to the sea for loading and unloading goods. In the old days these lodberries had been used for smuggling and it was said that passages from the lodberries led under the street to houses at the other side. Johnny thought it would have been exciting to be a smuggler and wanted to look for a passage. His ideas and ambitions were stamped on by grandmother, mother and aunts.

Obviously another source of amusement had to be found and in true Johnny fashion he found it. There was a grill in the floor of the house just in front of the toilet. Perhaps it had been meant at some time for ventilation for the cellar. Johnny and his accomplice Jean put it to another use. If they peered down through it, when there was no-one around in the house, they could spot when someone went underneath and drop small stones or spent matches on them. They spent a lot of time there, hitting some of the men and giggling when they looked up to see what had fallen on them.

It was inevitable that Hug would catch them one day as he walked through the front door. They were led by the ears down to the cellar to apologise to the men and a rug was nailed over the grill. They looked around for something else to occupy them and their eyes lit upon the graceful curve of the banister edging the staircase. They had been forbidden to slide down it, of course, but that meant little to either of them.

It was ill luck that sent Hug through the front door just as Jean climbed on at the top. The opening of the door unbalanced her and she toppled over and fell with a thump on her father's head, knocking him over. Before he could pick himself up Jean was through the front door and away. Hug knew he had been felled by one of them but which one he never discovered.

The streets of Lerwick at this time echoed to the clatter of wooden clogs. Dutch fishing boats filled the harbour and large Dutch fishermen walked the length of Commercial Street. The children were warned not to talk to them or to go with them. There were stories of young children being carried off to Holland, stories passed mostly from one youngster to another.

Cissie was five years old. Unlike the rest of the family she was dark haired. Because she suffered from asthma she was not as robust as the rest and looked like a changeling, a fairy child. On a day when the Dutch fishermen were ashore and walking through the streets, Jean and Johnny were sent outside to keep an eye on Cissie as she played. Along came a large and fat Dutchman who picked up Cissie. He was taken by her fey, dark looks and smiled at her. She smiled back. He offered her a peppermint. Most of the fishermen carried peppermints and a bottle of cologne that they would obligingly use to put on a hanky if asked.

Johnny started to yell. "Put her down! Put her down!" The Dutchman laughed and set off along the street in the direction of the harbour. Jean and Johnny ran after him screeching, "Put her down!" Then Johnny had a bright idea. "Kick him in the belly, Cissie," he yelled. "Kick him in the belly!"

Cissie paid no attention. She was enjoying herself, being carried along and fed peppermints. They reached the harbour, Johnny's voice hoarse from yelling. The Dutchman set Cissie down, gave her another peppermint and laughed as he turned towards his boat. Jean and Johnny grabbed Cissie and holding a hand each raced back along the street.

On Sundays the family went to church, to St Columba's. When the Dutch fishing fleet was in the harbour, the fishermen had their church service just before the local congregation and Jean thought it strange to see the steps of the church lined with rows and rows of clogs. She could never understand why they left their shoes outside. She also wondered how on earth they found the right pairs when they came out, but they seemed to know their own ones.

Sundays were different. Sunday was a day apart. No work was done and food was prepared the day before. Children were not allowed to play with toys or to play games. They could read if they liked, but this was a little tame for Jean and Johnny. They had discovered that they could pretend to be at Sunday School and many a riotous Sunday School was held on the stairs with Jean as teacher and the rest as a raucous choir. Somehow their parents tolerated the noise.

On one particular Sunday, while the Sunday School was in full cry on the stairs, Hug and Leebie were discussing the minister's sermon. It had seemed a little unusual.

Hug was laughing. "Did you hear him, Leebie?" he said.

"I did," said Leebie, "and I wondered what on earth he was talking about."

"You Shetlanders," quoted Hug. "When you pray, you pray for Shetland and the adjacent islands of Great Britain!"

"Well," said Leebie, "when I pray, I pray for the family first and then maybe Shetland. I don't bother with the rest unless they maybe need it."

"I'm sure he means that we think we are the centre of the universe here. That we think nobody matters except ourselves."

"What would give him that idea? We pray for the King, don't we?"

In 1910 a splendid new building had been completed to house the Post Office. The move was of no great distance, just barely fifty yards along Commercial Street, but as a place of work it was a huge advance. The staff revelled in the up-to-date surroundings and efficiency soared.

Jimmy Williamson was eighteen. He was enjoying his work in the brand new telegraph room and had become adept at telegraphic work. He was kept busy all the time and in the height of the herring season there was hardly time to sneeze between one cable and the next if he was on late shift.

"Lerwick," he thought, "is the herringopolis of the north." The brokers' cables, the ten-letter cipher cables of the German firm Braun and Megow and the rest, Finkelstein, the Dutchman Van Zevender, came rushing in just before the counter closed at 10.30 pm. These had all to be dealt with by the staff on duty as quickly as possible.

It was worse in the sorting office. On Monday mornings you might say the place was 'swarming' with work. Parcels of clothes from the Lowestoft and Yarmouth fishermen, their weekly wash being sent home, would practically jump into the mailbags themselves, they were so full of fleas from the drifters.

Jimmy did not have much free time at all. He had however managed to join the Territorial Force and played his part in this with his usual enthusiasm and blithe spirits. He got some training with guns as he had anticipated and target practice out at the Ness of Sound was a highlight. He had no thought of it being a useful skill to acquire. It was just fun.[1]

George Manson, meanwhile, was on his way home. He was now twenty-six and for the last three years he had been sailing, on one boat or another, from Australia to New Zealand and across the Pacific to San Francisco and the State of Washington, to British Columbia and back to Australia. He had seen many strange things and many sights were printed on his memory forever.

Perhaps the strangest thing of all about his travels was the frequency with which he encountered other Shetlanders. Or perhaps that was not so strange after all. Shetlanders are seafarers first and foremost. On ships or in ports is where you will meet them. At times it seemed as though half the able-bodied men in Shetland were on the sea; fishing, in the Merchant Navy or in the Royal Navy. Unkind people used to say that there were two kinds of Shetland men: the go-ahead ones who left to go to sea and let their wives do the work on the croft and the others who stayed at home and let their wives do the work on the croft.

George took a place on a ship bound for Europe. It was a different kind of vessel to the ship he came out on but he enjoyed doing the trip in reverse. When the ship reached Hamburg he left and made his way back to Shetland. He wanted to go home to see his parents.

---

1   From a letter from Jimmy Williamson to George Manson dated 19th May, 1957.

In 1910 Maj Evans was still in Hong Kong at HMS *Tamar*. He had finished gathering intelligence on several Chinese forts and had submitted his report for which he received an expression of their Lordships' appreciation for his work. He had now been instructed to gather information on the German South Pacific Islands.

CHAPTER 4

1911

GEORGE MANSON was home in Lerwick. His parents were delighted to see him again and he was settled for the time being. He thought he would go off on his travels again when the urge took him but for now he was content to stay at home and be with his family. He was pleased that he had come home in time to act as best man at his brother Willie's wedding and being at a Shetland wedding again made him realise that he had been missing the company, the music and the dancing. It was enjoyable, exhilarating.

His parents were keen to hear about his journeys around the globe and most interested to hear of all the Shetlanders he had met. Some of them they had known before they left Shetland. George had a very good memory and could recount his travels almost day to day. He had been away for three years but it seemed to him much longer. He had travelled so far and had seen so many strange things.

He slipped back into life in Lerwick as if into an old glove and looked around for some temporary work to tide him over and earn some money before he set off again. He thought he might find some employment as a telegraphist as he had lost none of his old skill. From the remarks dropped by his old colleagues the instrument room at the Post Office seemed to be busier than ever.

Word of his return had spread through the town and before he could approach the Post Office, he was approached by them and asked if he would consider working there on a temporary basis. This suited him very well and soon he was back at work, feeling as though his journey round the world had been a dream. At the back of his mind he kept the idea of once more setting off round the world and for that reason he continued as a temporary worker.

Some of the staff in the telegraph room were familiar to George. He had worked with them before. Hug Tait was there still. He was now an overseer, one of two. The other was Willie Stout. Hug and Willie were good friends. Willie had been best man at Hug's wedding, some ten years before. There were new faces though. He had not met Jimmy Williamson before. He seemed popular with the rest of the staff and certainly he had a good sense of humour. He kept them all lively.

One day Jimmy came into work with a long face. It was unusual for him to be anything but cheerful so it was not long before someone asked him what was wrong with him.

"It's the coronation," he said.

"Why on earth would that upset you? Should be the opposite! We'll get a day off work maybe."

William Stout in 1913.

Photo: Courtesy of Lerwick Post Office

"No, no," said Jimmy. "You don't understand. I joined the Territorials, remember?"

"Aye, we knew you were a 'moorit dreeller'."

"Well, they've been asked to send a detachment to London for the coronation. Captain Stephen is taking them."

"I heard that," said one of the staff. "Bob Mackay is going. I heard him telling one of the other postmen about it. He's excited about it. They have to dress up in full kit, kilts and all."

"It's great that they've been asked. What is there in that to annoy you, Jimmy?"

"I'm not going, that's what," said Jimmy.

"You couldn't expect to go. You haven't been in the force for very long. There will be a lot more than you disappointed."

"Oh, I suppose so," said Jimmy, sighing.

The detachment from the Territorial Force sailed on the boat to Aberdeen in the middle of June. A great crowd of townsfolk gathered on the pier to cheer them as they left. "Give our regards to the King and Queen," a voice shouted as the ropes were cast off. "We will. We will," was the reply and the wail of the pipes echoed over the widening strip of water.

Hug was still in the force. He had been made up to Lance Corporal and would have liked to go to London with the men but his job as overseer prevented that. Besides, another addition to the family was expected about the same time so he could not leave Leebie. In July, Leebie went into labour. Hug was fully expecting another girl and was duly surprised to find he had a son. They called him Andrew, after Hug's father.

The family in Lerwick saw Hug's father, whom they called Pa, quite often. His ship would come in carrying a cargo of this or that. It was his proud boast that he was the skipper who carried the sandstone from Eday in Orkney to Lerwick to build the town hall. Jean used to think it was their very own town hall, because Pa built it. They all loved Pa.

Jean was delighted to have a little brother at last and Johnny was just pleased to have an ally, he thought, against all these girls.

"Hurry up and grow," he said to the baby.

Maj Evans was still at HMS *Tamar*. There was a sense of urgency now in the instructions he was receiving. He stepped up his work on the German South Pacific islands. On 5th August 1911 he was appointed Lieutenant Colonel.

In October 1911, Winston Spencer Churchill was given the post of First Lord of the Admiralty by Prime Minister Herbert Asquith. The Government was alarmed at the growing naval competition from Germany. The German Navy had the most up-to date ships and equipment and it was beginning to be seen as a threat to British domination of the sea. Churchill considered it important to build up the British Navy and also to strengthen the defences within Britain. To this end he looked carefully at the existing defences and at sites he considered vulnerable.

The home ports for the German Fleet were mostly in the Baltic Sea and to gain access to the Atlantic the ships could use two different routes. A discussion of the likelihood of each route came to the conclusion that the passage round the north of Shetland would undoubtedly be preferred to trying to sail through the English Channel. As the preferred option for a safe anchorage for the British Navy was Scapa Flow in Orkney, the importance of defending Shetland became ever more urgent.

The information held by the Admiralty on Shetland was studied minutely by Churchill. Among the files he found a yellowing page of newsprint, the editorial written on the occasion of the visit of part of the Channel Fleet to Lerwick. He decided to send an enquiry to the Director of Naval Intelligence, Rear-Admiral Alexander Bethell, and on 31st October, 1911 he sent a minute asking for his views on establishing a wireless station on Shetland. He also wanted to know if it would be worth putting a small torpedo boat base there and ended with a question about the extent of German influence in the islands.[1]

On 2nd November, 1911 Bethell replied that there was no real necessity for a wireless station as in time of war Shetland would be the base for the 7th Cruiser Squadron. He thought that the cost of a torpedo boat base would prove too much and added that German influence was not very marked in the islands. There had been very few German ships there since 1904.[2]

---

1   Churchill Papers, CHAR 13/4/2.
2   Churchill Papers, CHAR 13/4/3-6.

CHAPTER 5

1912

IN JANUARY, Leebie's mother died. Jean and Johnny and Cissie were inconsolable. Their grandmother had been an integral part of their lives and they could not imagine being without her. In vain did Leebie and Jessie and Mattie explain that she had just gone to heaven. If she was there, they wanted to go too. The smaller ones were not so affected. They were just puzzled. Why was everyone so sad?

In April 1912 Lt Col Evans returned from HMS *Tamar*, Hong Kong, to the Portsmouth Division of the Admiralty. He had been summoned back to Special Service and his work in intelligence provided the key to this. Their Lordships had been appreciative of his report on the German Pacific islands and they now wished him to draw up a scheme for the organisation of an intelligence system for the Shetland Islands.

First Lord of the Admiralty Winston Churchill had been of the opinion that the British Fleet was a necessity but the German Fleet was a luxury and he saw no reason to change his mind. He saw the build-up of the German Fleet as a direct threat to Britain's mastery of the seas and shaped his policy around this. The coastal defence of Britain was to him of the first importance and he looked for a secure base for the home fleet.

In a discussion paper of 1912 the sea space lying between the northern extremity of Britain and the west coast of Norway had assumed critical importance in the event of an Anglo-German war.[1] It was felt that this would be the preferred route of German traffic as the English Channel presented much greater dangers. German vessels had frequently been reported visiting Norwegian harbours. This was seen as a desire on their part to acquire a thorough practical knowledge of the area and the visits to Lerwick were recollected in that connection.

'Under these circumstances,' the report continued, 'a British war anchorage and base of operations as near this area as possible has become an imperative requirement, and Scapa Flow is incomparably better suited for the purpose than any other harbour.'

In June Churchill sent a minute to the First Sea Lord, Admiral Sir Francis Bridgeman, and the Chief of Staff, Rear-Admiral Ernest Troubridge, on the defence of Orkney and Shetland.[2] He wanted to find out the strength of the Territorial Forces in the islands and was concerned about a possible German annexation of Shetland in the event of war. As he knew nothing of the islands or the people who lived there he was dependent on information supplied to him by Navy intelligence.

August found him writing another minute to the Chief of Staff asking for a report on the War Office's progress in developing the Territorial Force in Shetland. Churchill stated that it might be necessary for the Admiralty to help the War Office financially 'so as to procure an armed and well disposed population'.[3] The scathing editorial from *The Shetland Times* was uppermost in his mind. Without the loyalty and co-operation of the local people it would be hard to secure the defence of Shetland and without that it would be difficult to patrol the northern waters in time of war.

George Manson was still in Lerwick and still working on a temporary basis in the Post Office. He was content for the moment to stay there and was enjoying life, taking each day as it came. One day, he thought, he would set off on his travels again but for the present the job and the wage was enough. It was hard work. They were busy most of the time in the telegraph room and the contract with the Great Northern Telegraph Co. meant that they needed a far bigger staff than most Post Offices.

Hug had learned Danish so that he could understand the cables that were sent between Denmark, the Faeroes and Iceland, and some of the others were beginning to understand it as well. George could now understand it pretty well and it was

1   Discussion Paper of 1912. National Archives, ADM 116/1293.
2   Churchill Papers, CHAR 13/12/8.
3   Churchill Papers, CHAR 13/12/90.

certainly useful. They would probably have been sending some garbled rubbish otherwise.

Jimmy Williamson was now twenty, enjoying his job and enjoying life in general. His enthusiasm for the Territorial Force was as great as ever so it was with dismay that he heard the rumours that the Territorials, the 'moorit dreellers', were to be disbanded. Nobody knew how the rumour had started but many of the force were talking about it. Bob Mackay, the postman, was complaining that it was ridiculous.

"Fancy getting rid of the Territorials just a year after they asked us to go to the coronation," he said. "There's no sense in it."

"It's a rotten shame," said Jimmy. "I'm sure I would have got to go to the next one."

Hug listened to them. He thought too that it was a mistake to disband the force, just at the present time. If newspaper reports were to be believed there might be a threat to the Northern Isles from foreign powers. In that event the Territorials would be a useful weapon to have at hand.

In August Hug took his family on holiday. They went to Dunrossness as usual to Leebie's cousins. It meant a full day's journey with the pony and trap and it was viewed with great excitement by the children. It was viewed with trepidation by Hug and Leebie who eyed the weather anxiously. However on the Saturday when they set off the weather was fine. There was some cloud but it was clearing and it did not look as though it would rain. Family and luggage were packed into the trap and they left Lerwick heading south.

"Shetland roads!" said Hug. "If you're not going up a hill, you're going down, and if you're not doing either of those two things, you're going round a corner."

So it proved as they wound their way slowly towards Dunrossness. Whenever they came to a steep hill, which was fairly frequently, everyone got out except Leebie and baby Andrew and they walked up, briskly enough to begin with, full of holiday spirit. Jean and Cissie helped Joey along and Leebie dawdled behind as usual. At the top, they climbed back in and the pony stepped out brightly again on the downward slope.

There were cousins in Cunningsburgh and they stopped there for dinner. The table had been set for them in the best room. Leebie took them in and adjured them to be on their best behaviour.

"Mary has gone to a lot of trouble for us," she said, "so you must be good as gold now."

They all sat down and waited for Hug to say grace.

Through the open kitchen door, Jean could see the family sitting down to their own dinner at the table there. There would have been no room for all of them at the table in the best room, but Jean wished she could have been in the kitchen with the rest of the children there. They had plates in front of them of course, but no forks or knives. Instead they each grabbed a potato from one large dish and dipped it into another dish full of some kind of fish. Jean thought it must be salt fish, the same as they were having in the best room, but much more fun. No knives, no forks, just fingers. She looked longingly at them laughing and chattering amongst themselves, while in the best room they had to sit prim and proper and silent.

After dinner though there was a little time to play with the cousins, to be shown the pet animals and the cats and dogs.

"We only have a cat," said Jean. "It's a big one called Tom and we need it to catch all the rats in the lodberry and the yard."

"Ours catches rats too."

"Cissie puts dolls' clothes on it and puts it in the doll's pram."

"He's a very good cat, Tom," said their mother. "Very good at catching rats and he never steals anything. You can leave him in the kitchen and he won't take anything off the table."

"Hmm!" thought Jean, who had seen Tom coming out of a neighbour's kitchen window with a huge fish in his mouth. "He maybe doesn't take anything from us! But I remember Mrs Gilbertson wondering what had happened to her Sunday dinner."

Hug summoned them all back to the trap and they climbed in shouting thanks and goodbyes as they set off south again.

"These roads have not been here all that long," said Hug. "There was a man called McKenzie who came up here from Orkney to build them. He lived in Quarff I think. He was supposed to be a smuggler too."

"What did he smuggle?" asked Jean.

"Gin, I think," replied Hug. "Off the Dutch boats I suppose."

"Be exciting to be a smuggler."

"Not if you got caught," said Hug, sternly.

At the end of a long weary day, when Andrew and Joey were asleep already and Leebie was grumbling a bit that her feet were sore, Dunrossness came in sight and soon they reached the house and a fine welcome from Catherine Margit. Jean looked eagerly for Lowrie and fiery-headed young Catherine Margit and saw them running over the field towards the trap.

"You had a fine day for it, then," said Catherine Margit. "Come on in now. You will be hungry and tired."

They lifted the sleepy bairns and went inside.

In September Churchill received a memorandum from the Chief of Staff,[4] Admiralty, Sir Henry Jackson on the importance of developing the Territorial Forces in Orkney and Shetland to counter German influence and protect a naval wireless station on Shetland.

On 25th September Churchill requested that the memorandum be shown to General Sir John French, Chief of the Imperial General Staff.

In October a confidential letter was sent from the Admiralty to the secretary at the War Office expressing the disquiet felt by their Lordships at the proposal to disband the Territorial Forces in the Northern Isles.[5] They considered that the islands were extremely important strategically. 'In the Shetlands particularly,' the letter said, 'the detached situation of the islanders has tended to weaken their sense of British nationality.'

Their Lordships were worried about the frequent visits of the German vessels and the amount of German influence already obviously at work in the islands. They were so seriously impressed with the importance of Shetland to the national defence that they proposed to set up a naval wireless station there and this would certainly need protection from the outset. Therefore a Territorial Force would be necessary for this. The population of the islands should be organised into such a force. A strenuous effort should be made to induce as many of the people as possible in the islands to be associated with the British forces both by uniform and by retaining fee.

'It was probable,' the letter continued, 'that other steps will be necessary in the near future in order to secure the Shetlands and, in a lesser degree, the Orkneys, against an attempt at seizure by a coup de main before the actual outbreak of a war.'

The letter ended with an offer to assist the Army Council in representing to the Treasury the great importance of the matter from the point of view of the national security.

4   Churchill Papers, CHAR 13/13/84-86.
5   National Archives, ADM 116/1293.

CHAPTER 6

1913

IN MARCH Jessie Ann was born, the youngest of Hug's daughters. She was born prematurely and the family was worried about her health and Leebie's health. Jessie was small, certainly, but Cissie had been smaller still and she was fine now. As the days passed the anxiety grew less and although Jessie was a fretful baby, she slowly put on weight and grew stronger.

In the same month, Churchill was once again preoccupied with the question of the disbandment of the Territorial Forces in Orkney and Shetland. On 3rd March he sent a minute to Colonel John Seely, Secretary of State for War, on the importance to the Admiralty of the Orkney and Shetland Territorials and his disappointment that the War Office was preparing to disband these units.[1]

George Manson was still in Lerwick. He had not relinquished his dream of once more setting off on his travels but he was now friendly with a girl called Mary Henry and she was becoming more and more important to him. When he was offered a permanent position at the Post Office by head postmaster James Leiper he accepted readily.

An official photograph of the staff was taken. The result, after every member of staff had been inserted into a large shield and two views of Lerwick added at the foot, was approved by them all.

---

1   Minute – Churchill Papers, CHAR 13/22a/25-26.

LERWICK POST OFFICE STAFF.

1913

"This looks really good," said Jimmy Williamson. "Think I'll get one of these and put it in a frame. Then I can remember everybody who was here."

On 5th August a meeting of the Committee of Imperial Defence was held in London.[2]

2   Meeting of the defence committee – National Archives – ADM 1/8925.

The ninth item on the agenda was the defence of the Shetland Isles. Churchill was first to address the meeting on this topic. He spoke of the Admiralty's fears that Shetland might become an object of attack in the event of a war with Germany. He was concerned that, at the present time, they were undefended and dismayed that the War Office was hoping to disband the small body of Territorial troops which existed. He thought that the inhabitants had, in recent years, seen a good deal more of German warships than of British and that their attachment to Great Britain was somewhat weak. He therefore asked the War Office to protect them but the War Office seemed reluctant to do so.

Lord Haldane, the Lord Chancellor, thought it unnecessary as the Navy could quickly blockade them and protecting Shetland would mean that they would have to protect Orkney and the Hebrides as well and this would entail a huge expense.

The First Sea Lord, Prince Louis of Battenburg, demurred, saying that there were many excellent little harbours in Shetland which would be useful to an enemy and these would be seized, if at all, immediately on the outbreak of war. It was essential, therefore, that the defending force should always be there, otherwise it would arrive too late.

The Prime Minister invited the two senior Admirals present, Lord Fisher and Sir Arthur Wilson, for their opinions. They were in favour of basing some destroyers in the islands and of organising a proper military force there. There were a considerable number of excellent Royal Naval Reserve men there who could be associated with defence.

Sir Henry Jackson, Admiralty Chief of Staff, thought that what was required was a good and permanent system of intelligence and communications and a small but efficient local force on the spot.

The Secretary of State for War, Col Seely, objected to providing small amounts of troops. They would not object to improving the intelligence arrangements and organising the local forces although they did not agree with the policy.

The Prime Minister eventually summed up by emphasising that the organisation of a proper intelligence system and improvement in the arrangements for its transmission should be taken in hand at once.

The Chancellor of the Exchequer, Lloyd George, regarded the demands made by the Admiralty as serious and was not convinced of their necessity.

Mr Churchill said the Admiralty wished to place on record that they regarded the proper organisation of the defence of the Shetland Islands as essential and urgent.

In late September, the Prime Minister and Churchill were onboard the Admiralty yacht *Enchantress* on a cruise, with their wives, round the north of Scotland. They sailed through Scapa Flow and tied up at the pier at Scapa. From there they went to Kirkwall, walking through the town and visiting the cathedral. On their return to *Enchantress* they set sail for the Western Isles.

On 30th October the staff of the Post Office in Kirkwall gathered in the Kirkwall Hotel to say farewell to the postmaster, James Macmaster.[3] He had been in Kirkwall for about four years and had reorganised the office there and increased its efficiency. The staff were truly sorry that he was leaving and, after a sumptuous meal, there were many tributes from those present. There had been a flood of letters and cables from all of the sub-Post Offices also. Overseer John Firth made the opening speech and then called on Mr P S Campbell to present Mr Macmaster with an address, which had been designed and prepared by Mr G Sinclair of the Burgh Surveyor's Office. The address was in the following terms:

February 1910 – October 1913

To James Macmaster, Esq.
We, the members of the indoor and outdoor staffs of the Kirkwall Post Office and sub-Post-Offices in Orkney, desire, on the occasion of your promotion to the Postmastership of Lerwick, to place on record our appreciation of your unfailing courtesy and tact, both in your official and private relations with us. Your period of administration has been a most trying one in consequence of the very considerable increase of business, occasioned not only by the abnormal development of the postal and telegraph work, but by the National Insurance Act. Notwithstanding this, the arrangements made by you have invariably given entire satisfaction, not only to the staff under your control, but also to the general public. We regret exceedingly that your official connection with us is being severed, but we assure you that your memory will be long treasured by us all, and we shall watch with warm interest your future career, which we feel confident will be a brilliant one. On behalf of the respective departments we subscribe ourselves respectfully, JOHN FIRTH, on behalf of the indoor staff;

---

3   *The Orkney Herald*, 5th November, 1913.

James Macmaster in Auckland, New Zealand in 1934.

Photo: John H Manson

W.C.CLARKE, on behalf of the outdoor staff; D.W.MUNRO, on behalf of the sub-Post-Offices.
Kirkwall, 30th. October, 1913.

Mr Macmaster and his wife, Elizabeth, left Kirkwall for Lerwick on the following Saturday.

"I was sorry to see Mr Leiper leave," said Leebie. "Do you think this new man will be as fine to work for?"

"He seems to be a very fine man," replied Hug. "He is taking a lot of interest in the staff. Says he wants us all to work together and to let him know if we have any complaints or any ideas that might help to make things easier. He is certainly very easy to talk to."

"Well, that's good," said Leebie. "I wonder what his wife is like."

"Oh! We have met her too. She came into the Post Office to meet us all. A very nice lady. I think we have been very lucky to get them here. I believe that Kirkwall were very upset to lose Mr Macmaster. He was there for about four years. I hope he stays here longer than that."

James Macmaster settled in quite quickly into his new position. He liked Lerwick and found the staff friendly and easy to work with. The new Post Office building was pleasant and made for efficiency. He was looking forward to his stay in Shetland.

He liked to keep up with what was happening in the rest of Scotland and therefore took *The Scotsman*. As it was a daily paper more than one copy would arrive at a time. When he had read them through, he passed them on to the rest of the staff and so it was that, in the end of November and the beginning of December, Hug found himself reading about a strange incident in Germany, in the province of Alsace.[4]

The first reports were puzzling. Apparently a young German officer had insulted the local people of the town of Zabern in Alsace and there had been demonstrations hostile to the German government. It seemed as though the Alsatian government was going to resign in protest. As he read on Hug realised that the attitude of the military towards the local population had led to a serious situation.

The first days of December brought more information on the subject. A large number of people had been arrested and imprisoned overnight simply because a

---

4   Zabern incident – *The Scotsman*, 29th November, 1913; 1st, 2nd, 6th , December, 1913;
      7th January 1914.

schoolboy had hurled an insult at one of the soldiers. Included in this number were two magistrates and the public prosecutor. The whole affair was escalating out of control and had reached the highest levels of government. The Alsatian deputies in the Reichstag were demanding the removal of the regiment from Zabern.

The Scotsman certainly seemed to think that the military had exceeded their remit. The article implied that there had been a misuse of military power amounting to aggression and bullying.

Later Hug asked Mr Macmaster if he had read the articles on Zabern.

"I have indeed," said Mr Macmaster. "In a way it is just what you would expect of the German army. The officers are mostly Prussians and they do seem to think that they can do what they like."

"It seems to have started over something very trivial," said Hug.

"Yes. Got out of hand very quickly. Thank goodness that kind of thing can't happen in this country. British officers have more sense than that."

Hug continued to follow the Zabern saga for some weeks. It rumbled through December and into January.

On 10th December Hug's family were celebrating a wedding. Leebie's sister Jessie was married to Alex Fox and Johnny acquired a stepfather. They were to live in Gas Cottage as Alex worked for the Gas Company. Gas Cottage was away at the north end of Commercial Street, beyond Fort Charlotte.

"That's miles away," said Jean. "We'll never see you."

"Don't be daft," said Johnny. "I'll be here every day still. See if I'm not!"

COMMITTEE OF IMPERIAL DEFENCE.

EXTRACT FROM THE MINUTES OF THE 124TH MEETING HELD ON 5TH AUGUST, 1913.

9. DEFENCE OF THE SHETLAND ISLANDS.

(C.I.D. Papers 57-A, 58-A, 59-A.)

MR. CHURCHILL said that the Admiralty considered that the Shetland lands were very important strategically in the event of war with Germany. So uch so that they thought it conceivable that they might constitute an objective for tack immediately on the outbreak of war. At the present time they were undefended, d the War Office proposed to disband the small body of Territorial troops which tually existed. The inhabitants had in recent years seen a good deal more of rman and Norwegian warships than of British, and the Admiralty had been led to lieve that their attachment to Great Britain was somewhat weak. The Admiralty d therefore asked the War Office to protect the islands against a *coup-de-main*. e War Office apparently found great difficulty in arranging to do this. The miralty were very reluctant to assume responsibilities outside their sphere, but if e responsibility for the defence of these islands was laid upon them, they were pared to put forward definite proposals. The general scope of these was icated in the Admiralty Memorandum (C.I.D. Paper 58-A.).

Part of the minute of the Committee of Imperial Defence regarding Shetland.

National Archives at Kew.

CHAPTER 7

1914 (April to October)

IN APRIL Hug left the Territorial Force. He was awarded the Territorial Force efficiency medal. Leebie was inclined to think that being awarded a medal was quite grand but Hug was more realistic about it.

"It's just for the length of time I've been in it," he said. "If you serve twelve years, then you get one. Nothing grand about it."

"Still, it's a medal," said Leebie. "Something to show for the hours you put in, I suppose."

Throughout the first months of 1914 there were rumours of war. Memories of the Boer War were still fresh but it had had little effect on the Northern Isles. It was felt however that this was more serious. The threat was coming from Europe and Britain had not been actively involved in war in Europe for a hundred years. Anxiety grew.

In the last days of July, Sub-Lt Geoffrey Hughes-Onslow began writing a diary on board HMS *St Vincent* commanded by Captain Fisher.[1] A signal had been received that all leave was cancelled. He and his fellow officers considered it likely that there was trouble brewing in Ireland but they were then informed that Austria was mobilising against Serbia. The ships were ordered into Portland Harbour and he noted in his diary that they took on coal, filling up to 'peace stowage'.[2]

The following day they heard that Austria had declared war on Serbia. He duly wrote that the fleet at once proceeded to raise steam. During the following days Sub-Lt Hughes-Onslow's diary recorded the Fleet's movements until, on Saturday 1st

---

1   Excerpts from unpublished diary of Sub. Lt. G. Hughes-Onslow.

2   Peace Stowage: more cargo was allowed in time of peace, therefore the ship was lower in the water

August, the Fleet reached Scapa Flow accompanying the flagship *Iron Duke* with Admiral Sir George Callaghan onboard. On that day he recorded that the general opinion was that war was inevitable and added that guns were being mounted on the ship.

By the beginning of August it became obvious to all that war was indeed inevitable. Churchill set in motion the plan for the blockade of Germany's exit to the Atlantic and ordered Rear-Adm Dudley R S de Chair to take command of the 10th Cruiser Squadron and make his way north to Shetland and his base at Swarbacks Minn. This was to form the Northern Patrol to stop and search shipping around Shetland. The ships were all ageing cruisers but they were to become an effective force.

Lt Col Evans had arrived in Shetland and on 2nd August he mobilised the Royal Navy Reserve.[3] They were gathered by the next day in Lerwick. The members of the Shetland companies, the Territorials, were also summoned. A list had been made in advance of those who would be required to guard the telegraph huts around Shetland. These men were now sent to do this duty and Jimmy Williamson said goodbye to his friends in the Post Office and set off in his usual cheerful fashion on this new adventure.

War was declared on 4th August.

On that day Rear-Adm de Chair was sailing up the west coast of England aboard HMS *Crescent* on his way to Swarbacks Minn in the north of Shetland. On that day also Admiral Jellicoe was appointed to supreme command of the Navy and Rear-Admiral C E Madden was appointed his Chief of Staff.

On 8th August Parliament passed the Defence of the Realm Act. This gave the government unprecedented emergency powers to take over land and businesses deemed necessary for the prosecution of war. It made it an offence to communicate with the enemy in any fashion and it also conferred on the Admiralty and the Army Council and the members of His Majesty's forces the authority to arrest and punish people breaking the regulations.

In his diary, Sub-Lt Hughes-Onslow recorded on that same day that a light cruiser squadron was dispatched to investigate a suspected submarine base in Fair Isle but that the weather was too bad to make a landing. The next day he wrote that the cruiser *Birmingham* had rammed and sunk enemy submarine U15 near Fair Isle and that a landing had been made on Fair Isle but there was no trace of any base.

---

3   Lt. Col. Evans' career details – National Archives, ADM 196/62.

Members of the Sandwick cable guard group next to the parish church. Cable guards were soldiers of the Shetland Companies, Gordon Highlanders, responsible for guarding the landfalls of the telegraph cable to Shetland at places such as Sandwick, Burwick and Belmont.

Photo: R Ramsay, Shetland Museum and Archives Photo Library

A Royal Navy steam yacht in Lerwick Harbour, thought to be HMY Shemara. The picture was taken some time between August 1914 and March 1915. Shemara was the headquarters of Senior Naval Officer Cdr Startin.

Photo: Shetland Museum and Archives Photo Library

On 11th August his diary entry contained reports of aircraft sighted. He wrote that the ship was 50 miles west of Shetland and that they saw no craft whatsoever but that his watch had been made interesting by the huge numbers of seabirds which they passed. His diary went on to record:

"The Captain, addressing the hands, said that it is considered not improbable that the Germans have a base for torpedo craft, submarines and aeroplanes somewhere in Shetland, and that it is known that for some years they have taken a more-than-fatherly interest in the welfare of these islands. Vice-Admiral Sir George Warrender states, in a signal to the C-in-C that some of the Shetlanders are possibly sympathetic towards our enemies but from what little I know of the inhabitants of these islands this would surely be a gross libel."

The Admiralty yacht HMY *Shemara* was anchored in the harbour at Lerwick at this time. This was the headquarters for the Senior Naval Officer, Commander Startin, in charge of the naval base at Lerwick.

John Morrison was home on leave. He belonged to Lerwick and had gone to work as an officer in the Prison Service in Scotland. He had come home to see friends and family and was thus in Lerwick when war broke out. The local prison officer was a sergeant in the Territorials and about to be mobilised. The Prison Service realised with relief that they had a qualified man on the spot and instructed Morrison to take over. It suited him very well to stay where he was for the present.

Later in August there were newspaper reports of the arrest of spies in Belgium. Some 2000 people were said to have been arrested after the outbreak of war.

Almost every paper had further reports of spies. They were to be seen everywhere. In October a stranger was spotted in Caithness driving a large car. He was seen to take photographs and when his car was inspected it was found to be full of petrol and to contain, among other things, binoculars and maps. The stranger, who was foreign and spoke with a German accent, was arrested and the papers had a field day. Many of the details reported were invented and indeed the man finally proved to be a *bona fide* traveller for an English firm.

But such was the climate of suspicion at the time that the incident was exaggerated out of all proportion and even after his innocence was established people were still inclined to believe him guilty.[4]

4   Spy stories – *Orkney Herald*, 28th October and 4th November, 1914.

Warder John Morrison, who was on leave from the Prison Service in Scotland at the time of the incident.

Photo: Courtesy of Jimmy Winchester

Lt Col Evans was making his presence felt. As usual with an officer, he carried a cane under his arm as he walked round the town. Whenever he came across a member of the military or of the Territorial Force in the street, if a salute was not immediately given he would rap them over the arm with his cane and shout, "I'm waiting!" He seemed to have a compulsion to assert his importance.

On 2nd September there was a celebration. George Manson and Mary Henry were married. It was clear for all to see how happy they were and George's colleagues started to pass round the hat to buy them a wedding present.

The telegraph room in the Post Office had been a busy place before war had been declared. Now there did not seem to be enough minutes in the hour for the amount of traffic flowing through, and the number of staff had fallen with the removal of those who were serving in the Territorials. All the staff were working extra shifts, sometimes late into the evening.

Quite often when they were busy with telegrams they would hear the clink of cups and soon Mrs Macmaster's voice calling to them to come and have a cup of tea. She and her maid carried baskets from home laden with scones and flasks of tea. They were a welcome sight on a busy evening.

"I don't know how we will cope," said Hug, sinking into a chair beside the fire in the evening.

"Can you not get some of the men back?" asked Leebie.

"I doubt it. They have to go where they are sent in war."

"Well, you will manage as you always have," said Leebie comfortably.

"I suppose so. We must, at any rate. When the country's at war we all have to do whatever we can."

On the last day of October, Saturday 31st, Mr Macmaster received a telegram from headquarters which puzzled him a little.

"They are asking what staff are needed at Lerwick," he said to Hug. "We don't need any staff. I admit we are extremely busy in the telegraph room, but we can manage, can't we?"

"Yes, we can manage," said Hug. "The men are being very good about working extra hours if need be, since we lost some of the telegraph men."

"Well, then I will just reply that we have all the staff we need," said Mr Macmaster.[5]

---

5   Letter from Mr Macmaster to George Manson.

CHAPTER 8

Sunday, 1st November, 1914

SUNDAY was cloudy and dull. It was Communion Sunday and many of the people of Lerwick were at the Parish Church. George Manson and his new wife Mary, however, were at home. George had been advised to stay off work for a few days, as he had been unwell with rheumatism. Hug and Leebie Tait had gone to the Parish Church, and noticed that Lt Col Evans was there with some members of the Royal Naval Reserve.

HMS *Sappho*, an old cruiser stationed at Scapa Flow, arrived in Lerwick harbour while the communion service was in progress and a tender went from it to HMY Shemara carrying an officer. On board *Shemara* he handed a letter to Commander Startin, who opened it and read it intently.[1] The letter was from Sir Stanley Colville, Vice-Admiral of Orkney and Shetland, with instructions to detain all of the staff of Lerwick Post Office for questioning.

"This is a very serious charge," he said. "I must get hold of Lt Col Evans at once and get him to act on it. I had better go ashore and find him."

He discovered, when he inquired on shore, that Evans was at the Communion Service at the Parish Church and went there to wait for him. When the service finished and the congregation filed out many curious glances were directed at Evans and the naval officer. Evans read the letter and looked at Cdr Startin.

"Right," he said. "I know how to deal with this. Leave it to me. I've dealt with this kind of thing before. Let's go and make some arrangements. We will need to consider where we should put all these people."

He marched off, Cdr Startin following anxiously behind him. The congregation scattered homewards, excitedly discussing what his words had meant. Was there

---

1   Confidential report by D. Crombie, Inspector of Prisons – National Archives of Scotland (NAS), HH31/17.

going to be an invasion? Were some of his troops in trouble? They were all local men so they could not be guilty of doing anything, surely. The talk continued in their homes and many eyes watched for developments.

Lt Col Evans's first act was to summon members of the RNR and order them to tell all members of the Post Office staff to report to the Post Office without delay. He suggested that they first inform the overseers who would know how to get in touch with the rest of the staff. He then posted some men outside the Post Office to make sure that none of the men on duty tried to get out and to ensure all the staff were gathered in one place.

Jimmy Williamson, now Lance Corporal, who had been mobilised with the Territorial Force on 5th August, was home in Lerwick from Gutcher in Yell where he had been posted.[2] He had been sent back to Lerwick to form a class of signallers as there were none at headquarters. He had had a meal at the Territorial Hall at midday and then went to visit his parents in Mounthooly Street, where he had another dinner.

His father, who was a baker, had been at the bakery setting the sponge for the following day and when he came home at dinnertime he was looking puzzled.

"Something's happened at the Post Office," he said. "There's a sergeant on the door and a crowd of people around the place. Somebody said something about a spy."

"Come on!" said Jimmy to his brother Bob, who was a postman. "We'd better go down."

At the foot of the lane they met Charlie Arthur, a telegraphist from the Post Office. One look at his face told them something serious had happened.

"What's happening, Charlie?" asked Jimmy.

"I don't know," said Charlie. "Come on, Bob, they're calling in all the staff. You'd better come in."

Charlie and Bob went in. Jimmy stayed, watching. The crowd swelled as, in ones and twos, the staff of the Post Office arrived and disappeared inside the building. Rumours multiplied in hushed tones.

At 1.30 pm Lt Col Evans arrived at the county prison.[3] He demanded to see the warder in charge. When Warder Morrison appeared Evans asked him how many

---

2   Jimmy Williamson's own account, given in an interview for Radio Shetland.
3   D. Crombie's report as above.

prisoners he could take in. Morrison looked at him in surprise and said that there were eight empty cells.

"You will have to make room for more," said Evans. "Probably about 25."

"I am just going off for my dinner now," said John Morrison.

"Well, you can't go just now," said Evans. "The prisoners will be up in about a quarter of an hour."

"Well, what kind of prisoners are they? What are they charged with?"

"I can't tell you that. That is confidential. I am acting on confidential Admiralty instructions."

With that, Evans marched off. Morrison stared after him in bewilderment. He had fifteen cells at his disposal but he already had six male prisoners and one female with a baby, as well.

"Right," he thought. "If I am going to have as many as this, I need King back here."

Warder David King was on military duty about two miles away. Morrison sent off a message and instructed the bearer to be as quick as he could.

Meanwhile George and Mary Manson heard the doorbell clanging. George went to answer it and found one of his colleagues on the doorstep, looking grim. Before he could say anything his friend said: "You have to come on duty immediately."[4]

"On duty immediately?" said George. "I like that! The medical officer certified me suffering from muscular rheumatism on Friday afternoon and instructed me to remain indoors and keep warm until he saw me again, and now I am ordered on duty immediately. What's the matter anyway?"

"I can't tell you. Come over at once and you'll find out."

George went back to Mary and told her what had been said.

"I've a good mind to take the doctor's advice and stay home, but I suppose I had better go and find out. It's no distance anyway. I'll be back soon."

When he got out onto the street George was surprised to see so many on the move. Sunday was usually quiet but a great number of people were hurrying south along the street. He reached the Post Office and was astonished to find an armed sentry on duty with a sergeant of Marines acting as doorkeeper. The sergeant asked him if he was a member of staff. George nodded.

"Through there," said the sergeant and opened the door. The door locked behind him and George found himself confronted by another sergeant who directed

4   George Manson's articles.

Reading the latest telegrams during the early days of the 1st World War in Lerwick. The group includes soldiers of the Shetland Companies, Gordon Highlanders.

Photo: C Coutts, Shetland Museum and Archives Photo Library

EARLY DAYS OF WAR - READING LATEST
_TELEGRAMS AT NEWS-ROOM _ .

Sailors walking up Harbour Street, Lerwick, on 8th August 1914. Mobilising at Fort Charlotte, they were addressed by Lt Col H C Evans, who announced the formation of the RNR Shetland Section.

Photo: C Coutts, Shetland Museum and Archives Photo Library

him to the sorting office. Most of the staff were by now gathered there and were standing around in groups. On every face he saw a look of bewilderment.

Outside the Post Office Jimmy Williamson stood among the crowd, counting off the members of staff as they arrived and were herded inside. The crowd seemed in no mood to disperse and go home. The postmaster came down the lane, accompanied by a naval officer, and both were admitted into the building.

"Well," said Jimmy to the man standing beside him. "Maybe now we'll find out what it's all about and the men can get home again."

Some minutes later a detachment of the Royal Naval Reserve, headed by a sergeant, came at the double, south along the street from Fort Charlotte. They formed a semi-circle outside the staff entrance. Lt Col Evans arrived wearing his side-arms and the crowd stared in disbelief. He did not usually carry a weapon. He too vanished into the Post Office.

The staff had greeted the arrival of the postmaster with relief. At last they would find out why they had been summoned and the overseers, Hug Tait and Willie Stout, hurried across to ask him. The feeling of uneasiness returned as it became clear that Mr Macmaster was no wiser than the rest of them and the staff looked anxiously on as the postmaster was led through to his own office by Cdr Startin.

Macmaster found Evans sitting at his desk and stared in amazement.

"What is the meaning of all this?" he asked. "Just what is going on?"

"Sit down," said Evans, nodding to a chair.

"Why have you gathered all of my staff and indeed myself here on a Sunday," repeated the postmaster.

Evans looked at him searchingly.

"I have received confidential orders from the Vice-Admiral at Scapa Flow to detain and question the staff here," he said.

"For what reason?"

"I will tell you and trust you not to repeat this," said Evans. "The orders say that secret correspondence for the Fleet, passing through the Lerwick Post Office, has been tampered with and I have been ordered to detain the staff pending investigations."

"This is totally ridiculous," said Macmaster. "None of my staff would do anything like that. They are all completely reliable and trustworthy."

"Well, we shall see," said Evans, "but I have my orders and I must carry them out."

With that, he rose abruptly and went out of the room. He searched the whole building, making sure that all the staff were gathered in the sorting office and when they had all been accounted for he instructed one of the sergeants to line them all up.

The uneasiness among the staff grew when Evans burst through the door and they stared in disbelief at the revolver in his hand.

"Right," he said at full volume, waving his revolver along the line of men, "I am detaining you all on the authority of the Defence of the Realm Act, clauses 12 and 13." He read out the relevant clauses and then said: "I can't pick out the guilty one. Therefore I am scooping you all into the net. Away you go, now, and don't give me any trouble."

"Guilty of what?" said a voice from the ranks.

"Silence!" shouted Evans. "Take them away, sergeant!"

The sergeant stepped forward and marshalled them out into the street. He handed them over to another sergeant who herded them between two lines of RNR ratings standing with fixed bayonets. They saw the postmaster gazing at them in consternation as he stood in the doorway beside Cdr Startin.

Evans came out of the building and told the sergeant to take them away. The street was packed with people, staring in silence as the order "Quick march!" was given and they were marched away. One of the staff, Davie Gunn, was cripple and walked with a stick but he got no concessions from the sergeant and was forced to march along with the rest. The colonel followed them.

Jimmy Williamson watched in dismay as the column went north along Commercial Street and then turned left up Bank Lane. Where were they going? And why? Speculation was rife among the crowd. Some followed to see where the men were being taken, but Jimmy went home. He had to tell his mother and father what had happened to Bob.

No-one among the staff could believe what was happening. It was like something out of a nightmare. They were being herded along between lines of armed men with no idea of their destination. As they went along the Hillhead they wondered if they were headed for Fort Charlotte, but when they passed the Town Hall it became evident that they were going to jail. The gates of the county jail stood open and they were met by Warder Morrison. It was 3.55 pm.

Evans handed them over to the warder.

"They are not to be treated as prisoners," he said, "but as persons under arrest and they are to be granted every privilege."

He signed and handed over a letter, dated 1st November, as authority to receive and detain the men.[5]

LERWICK, SHETLAND ISLANDS
Sunday, 1st day of November 1914.

J.R.G.Morrison,
Warder in charge,
H.M.Prison, Lerwick.

You are hereby authorised and directed to receive and to keep in your custody the undernoted officials belonging to the Staff of the Lerwick Post Office also the mail gig-drivers until you get my authority for their release. I have also authorised that meantime food and bedding be sent from their homes in Lerwick to meet their requirements while in prison. -

James Macmaster (Postmaster)	Thomas L. Sinclair
James J. Tait	Robert Mackay
William Stout	James J. Robertson

5   Letter authorising arrest – NAS, HH31/17.

William A. Thomson
Thomas Pottenger
Joseph P. Sutherland
Robert B. Blance
Andrew P. Hawick
William G. Grant
John M Shed
George William Manson[6]
Andrew J. Nicolson
James M.C.Johnstone
John L. Anderson
John M. Arthur
David Gunn
Alfred Hay
Andrew B. Jamieson
Robert Stout

Robert Paton
John Johnston
Alexander Mackay
Robert Williamson
William H. Arthur
Frank Simmons
John S. Shewan
Andrew G. Garriock
John Mackay
John MacLennan
William Spanswick
Charles M. Arthur
George Hood
John Weir
Archibald J. Nicolson
Andrew M. Mouat
Hector Macrae (admitted 2/11/14)

(Sgd.) H. C. Evans
Lieut.Col. Officer Commanding H.M.Forces in Shetland Islands

The armed detachment then left them at the gates and Warder Morrison gathered them all together inside the prison.

"At dinnertime today," he said, "I received instructions from the military to be prepared to receive 25 or more prisoners almost immediately. Who they were or from whence they were coming was not divulged. Therefore I was greatly shocked as soon as I saw you chaps being marched along under armed guard. I am glad I know many of you. I went to school with some of you, and as long as you are under my care I promise you that not a key will be turned against you, and you shall have complete freedom of movement throughout the day. But remember! Should anyone betray the trust I'm placing in you I shall be the one to suffer."

He took them up to the exercise loft, brushing aside their words of thanks and promises to be on their best behaviour. There they were left alone for a considerable time, making themselves as comfortable as they could on makeshift seats.

---

6 George Manson's middle name was the only one which Evans gave in full – and he got it wrong. His middle name was Walter.

Jimmy Williamson had gone back to headquarters, after he had seen his parents, to see if anyone there knew what was going on. He had just gone inside the hall when someone came running from the prison to ask if the warder could borrow some benches.

"We don't have enough seats for them all," he said. "They are up in the exercise room just standing about. We need something for them to sit on."

Jimmy grabbed hold of one of his colleagues.

"Here," he said. "You take one end of this bench and we'll go up with it."

When they reached the prison they set the bench down in a corner and Jimmy ran up the stairs to the exercise room. He found his way barred by an iron grill, but he could see the staff, his friends, milling about behind it. Hug Tait spotted him and shouted over to him.

"Oh! Jimmy, here," said Hug. "Could you manage to tell the wife that we're all right and I think it will be all over in a day or two. Tell her not to be too anxious."

"Right, Mr Tait," said Jimmy. "I'll see that she gets the message."

Mr Macmaster looked at Cdr Startin after watching his staff being marched away, he knew not where.

"I want to know what is going on here," he said. "What does he mean by secret orders being tampered with?"

"I'm afraid I can't tell you," said Startin. "We are acting on confidential instructions."

"Am I being accused of something? Is one of my staff accused of something? Or all of them? Just what is all this?"

"I'm sorry. I can't tell you," replied the commander. "Now, I can offer you accommodation on the *Shemara* until things are cleared up. If you would like to come with me now."

"No," said Mr Macmaster. "I want first of all to find out where my staff have been taken."

"I can do that," said the commander. "Come with me."

"Can I go and inform my wife of what has happened?" asked Mr Macmaster. "She will be anxious no doubt."

Cdr Startin accompanied Macmaster to his house and waited while he informed his wife of what had happened.

"All of the staff have been arrested by the military," he said.

"What!" exclaimed Mrs Macmaster, her face turning white. "Why?"

"Apparently some secret orders have been tampered with."

"How? Is it supposed to be the telegraph room?"

"No, no," said Mr Macmaster. "No, it must be the mail. They must have lost a letter or something, or letters."

"None of your staff would do that."

"Of course not. They must have lost it themselves or never sent it. Or it's sitting on a desk somewhere. The whole thing's ridiculous."

"What are you going to do?"

"I'm going to see where they have been taken. Startin has offered me accommodation on the *Shemara* but I will probably stay with the men, depending where I find them."

Cdr Startin then led the way to the prison. When Mr Macmaster realised that his staff were in jail, he demanded to be allowed to join them.

"If my staff are in prison, then so am I," he said.

The commander made no objection. At 4.30 pm the postmaster reached the jail and the commander handed him over to the warder.

"What are you being charged with?" asked Warder Morrison. "There is nothing in my letter to tell me."

"I cannot tell you," said Mr Macmaster. "I was ordered to go to the Post Office and I was told that they were acting on confidential instructions from the Admiralty."

"Well, it's all very irregular," said John Morrison.

Cdr Startin walked down to Fort Charlotte and joined Lt Col Evans who had just given orders to some of his men to search the homes of all those he had rounded up.

"I told Warder Morrison that I would order the families of these men to supply mattresses and bedding for all the prisoners," he said. "I will tell the men here to order them to take up bedding right away. They will also have to supply food."

James Macmaster joined the men in the exercise loft. They were pleased and relieved to see him, especially when he announced that he was remaining there.

"Gentlemen," he said, "I don't know why we are here or how long we shall remain, but here I remain until we are all clear."

This statement was met with murmurs of approval.

"Is there still a crowd of people outside?" someone asked.

"Yes," said the postmaster. "There are a number of people out there wondering what is going on."

"I think we should try and let them know that we are all right."

"How will we do that?" said another.

"We could sing. They would hear us."

"It's Sunday. We can't sing songs."

"No, but we can sing hymns and psalms. Come on. The 121st psalm."

The crowd waiting outside heard the men's voices singing *I to the Hills Will Lift Mine Eyes* and the sound swelled as their voices joined in. At the end of the hymn those inside the jail heard loud applause coming from those outside.

Jimmy Williamson went along to 12 Commercial Street. He knocked on the door and almost immediately Jean opened it.

"Is your Mam in?" he asked.

Leebie came to the door looking distraught.

"What is happening?" she said.

"I have a message from Mr Tait," said Jimmy. "He said to say that they are all right and that it will be all over in a day or two."

"What are they in jail for?" asked Leebie.

"Well, nobody knows," said Jimmy. "You know fine they will not have done anything at all, so they will all be out very soon."

Leebie did not look convinced, but she thanked Jimmy and he went home to his parents.

When he reached the house, he found it invaded by naval ratings who were searching every room.

"What on earth is going on?" he said.

"We have orders to search the houses," said one.

"What for?" asked Jimmy.

"Well, we don't know."

"Then how can you search for it?"

"Well, it might be a letter," said another. "We are not sure. We were just told to search. And to tell you that you must bring a mattress and bedding up to the jail. And you must also supply food for as long as your son is in jail," he said to Jimmy's mother.

"For goodness sake," said Jimmy, after they left. "This is all totally stupid."

Mary Manson opened her front door to find a detachment of naval ratings standing there.

"We've come to search your house," they said, "and to inform you that you have to supply a mattress and bedding for your husband and food for as long as he is in jail."

They marched in. Mary looked on in bewilderment, wondering what they were searching for. One of them pounced on a piece of paper with a list on it.

"Sergeant," he said. "Look at this!"

The sergeant looked intently at the list.

"Explain this," he said. "Who are all these people?"

"That's my list of people that we have sent wedding cake to," said Mary. "It's not long since we were married and I have just sent out the cake."

"Oh," said the sergeant, looking slightly crestfallen. "Well, that's it, I think. Don't forget about the bedding."

In Leebie's house, men were searching also. Mattie was there and Jessie too. She had heard the news and come to see if there was anything she could do. They stood watching helplessly as the men opened cupboards and drawers and rummaged through everything. One of them found a cache of letters in a drawer. He took them out and began reading them. Jessie immediately flew into a rage and tried to wrest them out of his hands.

Market Street from the Town Hall tower around 1904 showing (on the right, going down) the premises of R W Tait, cabinetmakers, the market green, Ganson Brothers, the Turk's Head public house, Zetland Aerated Water Co (the fizzy factory) and building contractor J M Aitken. In the foreground a prisoner can be seen breaking rocks in the police station yard.

Photo: J D Rattar, Shetland Museum and Archives Photo Library

"Those are mine," she said. "Nothing to do with the Post Office. Give me them." But the man read on stolidly. He eventually handed them back, saying that they were not what they were looking for.

When the men had left, Jean wondered why her aunt Jessie had been so upset, and how her letters could have been in the drawer and not at her own home. She asked her mother, but it was a long time before she found out. They were love letters and had been sent to Jessie by a merchant seaman who had been lost at sea. Jessie had left them behind when she married Alex as she did not want to upset him.

At about 5 pm Warder Morrison called one of the postmen to go downstairs. He followed the warder and when he was out of sight a voice was heard saying, "Well, that's number one away to his doom." He was only half joking. When the postman returned about ten minutes later, he was questioned anxiously.

"What did they want you for?"

"Oh, to take in my mattress and blankets," he answered.

Mattresses and blankets for the rest arrived at intervals after for most of the men. Four of them however were in lodgings in Lerwick and were obliged to use prison bedding and the postmaster refused point blank to have bedding brought from home.

"I do not see why family and friends should be obliged to bring bedding and food for us," he complained to Warder Morrison. "We are here through no fault of our own. We did not ask to come here. These things should be supplied by those responsible for putting us in here."

The warder supplied him with bedding.

"I have to tell you, though," he said, "if you do not have food sent in I can only supply you with prison food."

After he had described what that was, the men decided that they would rather have their families supply it.

At about 5.30 pm Warder King arrived to help.

"I am not sure what I can do," said John Morrison. "I have fifteen single cells. I have seven prisoners, six men and a woman and baby, already. Now I have thirty-four more to deal with and this Evans says there will be more. What do you think?"

"You can't put all the convicted men in one cell. You couldn't get them in!"

"No. Well, two cells for them and one for the woman and baby. That's three. Leaves twelve. And I had better keep one of those back in case there are more."

"Put the convicted men on the top flat and the woman on the lower one."

The warders settled their original residents into three cells, leaving twelve to house the newcomers, six cells on each flat.

"Number one cell on the top flat has a fireplace," said Warder Morrison. "We should put the postmaster and the two overseers in that. Then we can let the rest decide amongst themselves where they want to go."

"I'll get the prisoners to clean out all the cells before we move them in," said King.

Cdr Startin decided to leave the rest of the arrangements to Lt Col Evans and return to the *Shemara*. He asked him if all the men had now been arrested and what he proposed to do to interrogate them.

"There are still six men to arrest," said Evans. "I left two in the post office to look after things there for the time being until I could make other arrangements. Then there are the mail-gig drivers who won't be back in Lerwick until 10 o'clock. And there are two linesmen out in the country who won't be back until tomorrow. I'll get them then. Then we shall see what will happen."

Startin went back to the Admiralty yacht feeling a little worried. He thought on the whole Evans had been very efficient at rounding up the suspects and was handling the house searches well. However, he felt disquiet about the fact that he seemed to be concentrating more on the arrest and less on the necessary questioning of the staff.

Inside the prison, Warder Morrison was allocating cells, or as he tactfully referred to them, 'rooms'. Beyond specifying that the postmaster and overseers were to have room number 1, he gave no instructions on who was to go where. He left it to the men themselves to sort out between them who would share. The cells in the upper flat had to have four in each, one cell in the lower flat had four and two had three. That left one free for any others. Each cell measured 10 ft. by 8 ft. and was 9 ft. 6 in. high. There was scarcely room to lay out four mattresses.

Some of the cells held members of the same family. Brothers Charles, William and John Arthur had one cell. Robert Stout, however, was in a different cell from his brother. Willie Stout was an overseer and was therefore in cell number one. They were sons of the Provost of Lerwick and were worried about what their father would think about the day's events.

John Morrison went back and fore between the 'rooms' helping them to sort out their bedding and reassuring them that he would leave the doors open as long as possible.

Brothers Charles (top left), William (top right) and John Arthur (left) shared a cell.

Photos: Courtesy of Lerwick Post Office

Calls came for individuals to go down and receive food brought by family and friends. The Provost, Robert Stout, arrived with food for his two sons. When Willie and Robert came down, he asked them if they knew why they had all been put in jail.

"Surely you must have been given some reason," he said.

"We have not been told anything," replied Willie.

"Well, you must have been asked some questions at least."

"No. Not one," said Robert.

The provost went to see the warder but found that he was as ignorant of the reasons for the imprisonment as the men themselves.

"This is absolutely outrageous," said the provost. "I will lay this matter before the sheriff tomorrow morning. Meanwhile I am going straight down to Fort Charlotte to try and speak to Lt Col Evans."

At 7 pm a military escort arrived with George Hood. His colleagues immediately surrounded him, demanding to know what was happening at the Post Office. He could tell them nothing. He had left John Weir still there dealing with the telegraph room and Charles Manson, the telegraph messenger, was still there too. They were locked in and the guards were still on the doors.

"They have been searching all our homes," said George Manson. "Mary told me when she came in with my supper. They pounced on a list she had made. It was only a list of people we had sent wedding cake to, but they wanted to know all about it. It looks as if they are looking for a list or something."

"Or a letter," said another voice. "They read through all the letters they could find in the house."

Mr Macmaster, Hug Tait and Willie Stout listened to the chatter and were glad to see that none of the men seemed to be afraid or worried. They were mostly angry, indignant at the way they had been treated.

"I confess that I am rather worried," said Macmaster. "Lt Col Evans told me in confidence why he has arrested us all. I think in fairness I should tell you two that he said secret orders that passed through the post office here had been tampered with. He can only mean that a letter has gone missing or something. Most likely nothing at all to do with us but unfortunately under the Defence of the Realm Act they can lock us all up, with no explanation, for as long as they like. And there is nothing we can do about it."

"Yes," said Hug. "I know. I am worried about Leebie and the bairns."

"Please do not let this go any further. Warder Morrison has said we can write letters and send out. They have been ordered to read them by Col Evans, so …"

The postmaster became aware that not all of the men were cheerful. One at least was extremely upset. He was a lad of seventeen, a Post Office learner, and it was obvious that there was something very wrong. Willie Stout went across to him.

"What's the matter, Jimmy?" he said.

"Oh, Mr Stout, I heard they were searching everybody's homes and looking for letters," said Jimmy Johnstone. "I was writing to my girlfriend last night and I left the letter in my pocket at home and I thought they would read it."

"They won't tell anybody about it," said Willie.

"No, it's worse than that," said Jimmy. "I wrote a note to my brother asking him to get rid of the letter and I've just been questioned by one of the sergeants. He wanted to know what it was I was so keen to get rid of."

"Well, you're back here again so he must have been satisfied with what you told him."

"I suppose so. I don't think I can stand this, Mr Stout. I've never been away from home before and I miss my mother and father."

"Look," said Willie, "there's room in our cell for one more. You had better come in with us. Then it won't be so bad, will it?"

Mr Macmaster smiled and said, "Bring your bedding in here, Jimmy."

"We'll make room for you," said Hug.

Jimmy smiled a rather watery smile but they noticed that he became much happier almost immediately.

"You'd think," said Macmaster, "to listen to them, that the rest think this is some kind of soirée or something." And indeed there was chatter and laughter all along the corridor.

Warder Morrison came along the corridor, checking that the beds had been laid out as well as could be expected on the floors of the cells. He saw some friends he had been at school with and stopped to speak to them.

"I got the shock of my life today when I saw you lot arrive," he said. "I assumed when the military approached me about housing 25 or more prisoners that they would be German prisoners of war. I never expected to see the whole of the Post Office staff."

"We didn't expect to be here either," said one of his friends, gloomily.

"I tried to tell the officer that I didn't have room for so many," said the Warder. "I didn't have the beds or the cooking facilities for half that number but I was just banging my head against a brick wall. He wouldn't listen. He was adamant. I was told to pack as many men as possible into every cell and warned to see that none escaped. When he said that I was sure they must be Germans."

Jimmy Williamson went along to the Territorial Hall for roll call and parade at about 8 pm. The events of the day dominated the conversation and everyone seemed to have some bit of information to add. Without exception, all of them had a relative or friend in custody, and they knew the rest of them anyway.

Jimmy was surprised to be told, by Major Broun, who was in charge of the local Territorial Force, to remain behind and report to his office.

Jimmy Williamson in 1913.

Photo: Courtesy of Lerwick Post Office

61

"Oh, Lord," thought Jimmy, "I think they are going to put me in jail too maybe. After all I am a member of the staff."

He went through to the office and stood to attention.

"Lance Corporal Williamson," said Major Broun, "you are a member of the Post Office staff in Lerwick and you know the workings of it?"

"I've had some experience of it, yes, sir," said Jimmy.

"Well, you're a telegraphist?"

"Yes, sir."

"Now," said Maj Broun, "my orders from Lt Col Evans are that you go down at 9 o'clock tonight along with Sergeant Reid and take over the Post Office. There are two men in the Post Office who have been there all afternoon from the time the rest of the staff were arrested and now they'll be taken up to the prison by Sergeant Reid, and you are to carry on."

"With respect, sir, one man can't carry on a post office. No, sir, I can carry on to a certain extent as far as I am able to, but it's impossible to carry on the telegraph side of it by myself. I'll keep up communications as far as Service telegrams go; I'll do my best to do that until a relief staff arrives, but to look at commercial work would be utterly impossible."

"Well, these are my orders from Lt Col Evans. Captain Stephen will be in charge, Lt Mitchell will be there to assist and there will be thirty other ranks from the Territorial Force to help out."

Jimmy was dumbfounded. One man, himself, with a knowledge of the Post Office based on only two years' experience, to run it with the help of a bunch of people with no clue whatsoever. He had no idea how it would all turn out, but one thing was sure. It would be utter chaos.

He went down to the Post Office with Sergeant Reid and found Charles Manson there, a temporary telegraph messenger.

"What are you doing here at this time of night?" he asked.

"I've been locked in all day," said Charlie.

"Well, you'd better go away home," said Jimmy.

In the telegraph room he found John Weir, who came from Edinburgh.

"I thought George Hood was here too," said Jimmy.

"He was marched off about 7 o'clock," said John. "My turn now, I suppose. I've been keeping up traffic to Aberdeen. Best of luck," he said and disappeared with Sergeant Reid.

Jimmy stood in the room, aghast at what he was supposed to do. He was not alone but he might as well have been. There were other people there, from the Territorial Force, but they sat and watched him. There was nothing they could do.

Jimmy was the only telegraphist among them; the only telegraphist available in Lerwick that night to keep up communications with the outside world.

He found that the telegraphists in Aberdeen knew what had happened because George Hood and John Weir had told them but they did not say much about it. Jimmy worked on through the night.

At 9 pm John Weir arrived at the prison accompanied by Sgt Reid. He was expecting to find a scene of gloom and despair and was a little taken aback by the noise and hilarity. His arrival coincided with the departure of Warder King, who was going back on military duty.

"I'm going to ask if you can come here to help out while I have such huge numbers," said Warder Morrison. "Would you do that?"

"Yes, sure," said Warder King. "If you ask for me, I'll come as soon as I can."

Late in the evening Archibald Nicolson, a mail-gig driver, drove up to the post office with mails from the country districts. He noticed that Territorials were taking in the mail but thought little of it until Evans arrived on the scene.

"Are you Nicolson?" he asked.

"I am."

"I want you."

"Well, I'm here," said Archie.

"Come with me."

Archie replied that he had his horses to attend to. At that Evans threw his dog into the back of the mail-gig and stood on the back step in silence until Archie reached Ganson's yard where the mail-gigs were kept. Evans then ordered him again to come with him but Archie protested that he had to see to his horses.

"To hell with your horses!" yelled Evans, getting angrier by the minute. "Come with me!"

Just then Ganson's foreman, Willie Manson, came into the stable and advised Archie to go with Evans.

"I'll see to the horses," he said.

It was raining hard and Archie was wet through by the time he followed Evans into the charge room in the prison. He listened while Evans read a long statement about the arrest of the staff.

"I count you as one of the staff," he said. "You will have to go with them and remain with them." He finished by saying: "To hell with you."

Archie's clothes were wet through but a request to go and get dry clothes was summarily refused. He shivered as he followed Warder Morrison through to the cells, where he found Andrew Mouat, the other mail-gig driver, also soaking wet.

In a very short time they were both summoned downstairs again and found Mrs Ganson, wife of the mail transport contractor in Shetland, carrying dry clothes and bedding.

"I'll be back with your supper," she said. "I couldn't carry it all."

George Manson went to Warder Morrison and asked if he could see the Post Office medical officer.

"I was signed off work with muscular rheumatism," he said, "and I was supposed to stay indoors. Would it be all right to ask him about it? Then you would not be responsible for my health."

"Yes, certainly," said Morrison. "I will send for him. I need to send for Dr Yule too in any case, as I need to know that everything here is being done correctly. He will be here soon."

Dr Robertson duly arrived dressed in military uniform, as he was medical officer for the troops also. When he saw George he agreed that he should not have been put in jail, but said he would not be allowed to go home.

"If you want," he said, "I can have you transferred to the local hospital where you will probably have to put up with an armed guard sitting by your bed day and night."

"I'd rather stay here with my colleagues, I think," said George. "If I am sent to the hospital, it will only upset my wife and my family."

"I think you're right," said Dr Robertson.

"Let me see your daily statement," said Dr Yule when he arrived to Warder Morrison.

The totals on the statement read:

"Under detention – 38 from Post Office.

2 cells with three convicted prisoners each – 6.

1 cell with 1 female prisoner with child – 1.

Total at locking up – 45."

"Overcrowded" wrote Dr Yule firmly underneath.

Warder Morrison included Dr Yule's remark in his report to the Prison Commissioners in Edinburgh of the detention of the entire Post Office staff and the arrangements he had made to accommodate them.[7]

When the mattresses were rolled out onto the floor of the cells, there was no space between them. The lights in the cells barely penetrated the gloom so there was

---

7   Warder's report – NAS, HH31/17.

no hope of reading when they lay down and the lights had to go out at 8 pm in any case. In one of the cells, someone had had the bright idea of starting a story-telling competition and soon others joined in.

"I need my tobacco," said a voice.

"Hey," said another, "watch where you're putting your feet."

"Ow! Don't stick your elbow there!"

There were helpless giggles from others as they watched their colleagues writhing around.

The story-telling, the chatter, the laughter went on to 3 am when those who were trying to sleep got fed up and yelled "Shut up!" Eventually silence reigned.

In Commercial Street, lights glowed from the Post Office as Jimmy Williamson struggled to keep up with the telegraph traffic.

CHAPTER 9

Monday, 2nd November, 1914

EARLY IN THE MORNING, George Manson was heading for the washroom to beat the inevitable queue. He found he was not the first to have that idea. The colleague who had knocked on his door the previous day was there before him, still looking very gloomy.

"Cheer up!" said George. "This is no worse than the first long voyage I went on some years ago. The first few days out of sight of land was a bit depressing but that feeling wore off and I was soon enjoying myself. I tell you, after we have been in here six months we'll all be feeling quite at home!"

"Six months! Long before that they'll be carrying me out feet first!"

George went off whistling to wash. On his return he found the occasional warder, who had been on duty during the night, standing talking to some of the men. As was usual in Lerwick he was known to them all and friends with many of them.

"I am really sorry to see you all in here," he said.

"You don't need to feel sorry for us," said George, abruptly. "We've done nothing wrong and so we have nothing to fear."

"Oh, I wouldn't say that," said the warder seriously. "No, no, no, I wouldn't say that. You know someone has done something very wrong or you wouldn't be in here."

"Yes, sure," said George. "I agree. But," he added, "that 'someone' isn't in here, and is never likely to be." With that retort he turned and walked away.

"Jean," said Leebie, "you can take this basket up to your father on your road to school. It's his breakfast. I've wrapped the pot of porridge with some towels to keep it warm. I hope it will be all right."

"Fine," said Jean. "If I leave a bit early then I will get to school in time anyway."

"Maybe you can collect it on your way home for dinner," said Leebie, passing the back of her hand over her eyes.

"Will Cissie and Leebie be all right on their own?"

"They'll be fine. They can go with some of the rest of the bairns here."

Jean went up to the Hillhead and walked along to the prison. She was not sure where to go to hand in the basket but she found that she need not have worried about it when she got there. There were plenty of other people, adults and bairns, waiting to hand in breakfasts. She waited until her father's name was called and saw him coming down to collect it.

"Why are you in here, Daddy?" she asked.

"Well, we don't really know," said Hug. "But we'll probably find out what it is all about today and then they'll let us come home, I expect."

"Mam's crying," said Jean.

"I know, I know. But you just tell her not to worry about it. I'll be home soon."

Jean left, upset that her father had to stay there but sure he was right about being home soon. She walked back towards the school among a crowd of other children.

Jimmy Williamson had worked through the night in the Post Office on his own. True, there had been many other people round him but they had done nothing. There was nothing they could do. They had not been trained for work in the Post Office and in fact were worse than useless as Jimmy soon realised.

Capt Stephen had arrived and inquired of Jimmy to find out what he could do to help. He at least had the advantage of working in an office himself, although an office of a different kind. He was the agent in Lerwick for the steamship company.

Jimmy was finding it difficult by this time to keep up with the telegraph traffic and indeed was in contact solely with Aberdeen. The sub-offices in Shetland began to come on call by telegraph but there was nothing he could do about it. The telegraph room needed a huge staff and he was here on his own. Suddenly he remembered the other function of the Post Office.

"The mail," he thought. "What on earth am I going to do about the mail?"

There was mail due to go away by the steamer that evening and mail to come in from fifty sub-offices. There was no-one there with any knowledge of what to do except himself. He asked the telegraph office at Aberdeen to hold on for a little and went down to the sorting office to see what he could arrange.

Jimmy knew most of the men who had been sent to help him. He picked out two of them to keep the letterbox in the wall of the Post Office clear and showed them how to use the date stamp to cancel the letters. "You just keep doing that," he said. He sent another to empty the pillar-boxes round the town at certain times. And then he sought out Capt Stephen.

"I've got some of the men doing something about the mail," he said, "but the North Isles boat will be in at about 4 o'clock with mail and the sub-offices too. It will be hectic. We need a few more here that know what to do. Can you get in touch with the cable guard stations and ask for Peter Robertson and Jock Thomson. They're at Sandwick. And could you get Davie Tait – he's a good friend of mine – from Ulsta in Yell. He could come down with the *Earl of Zetland* when she brings the mail."

"I'll see what I can do. Right away," said Captain Stephen. "I will also have to see what I can do about getting a supply of stamps to sell as the public are clamouring to get in and post things. I am not going to open the office to the public until the afternoon – and then only for a couple of hours. It will be all we can manage. But how do I get the stamps?"

"You will need to get hold of Mr Macmaster for that," said Jimmy. "He keeps the keys to the safe. And he's in jail, of course."

Jimmy returned to the telegraph room and Capt Stephen went in search of Lt Col Evans.

Soon after breakfast Warder Morrison opened his door to find a number of elderly men on his doorstep.

"Ah, gentlemen, come in!" he said.

"You asked us to come round today," said one. "Now, what is all this we have been hearing?"

"Come along with me," said the warder. "I want you to inspect the cells and the number of prisoners I am having to accommodate in them."

The inmates looked on with interest as the Prison Committee walked round, stopping every now and then to ask questions about the way that the men were being treated. They all without exception praised Warder Morrison for the way he was dealing with the situation. Without exception too they agreed that there was nothing further he could have done to help them.

"I wonder," said one of the men, "if you could do anything about the gas lights in the cells. They are pretty poor. Not much better than a match really."

The Prison Committee inspected the lights and assured them that they would be seen to immediately. With that, they went away.

Captain Alexander Stephen in Gordon Highlanders dress uniform and wearing the George V Coronation Medal.

Photo: R Ramsay, Shetland Museum and Archives Photo Library

When Capt Stephen arrived at Fort Charlotte he found a group of naval ratings in charge of a sergeant waiting to report to Lt Col Evans. With them he saw a man whom he recognised as the post office linesman, Hector Macrae. He looked bewildered. He went into Evans's office to speak to him. He thought that Evans did not seem to be in very good temper, perhaps from the exigencies of the previous day.

"The public are wanting to post letters and parcels," said Capt Stephen. "I need to be able to issue stamps."

"I put you in charge there," said Evans. "Get on with it, man."

"I would indeed get on with it, as you say, if I only had the wherewithal to do it," retorted Capt Stephen. "But I do not have access to the safe, and the money and stamps are in it."

"Who has the key?"

"The postmaster."

"Right," said Evans. "Soon sort this out."

Evans marched up the road to the prison driving Macrae before him. When he arrived at the prison, he was met by Morrison.

"Ah! I am glad to see you here," said the warder. "I have been asked by the Prison Commissioners in Edinburgh to point out to you that the accommodation here is insufficient for the detention of this number of men, and there is a possible danger to their health because of this. I must request that you remove them to somewhere more suitable."

"I don't have anywhere else to put them," said Evans.

"Well, at least give me some estimation of how long I am expected to keep them."

"I don't know," said Evans. "My orders are to keep them under arrest pending investigation."

With that, he handed Hector into custody and demanded to see the postmaster. Morrison went and fetched him.

"Give me the keys to the safe," said Evans. "They need to get some stamps."

"I'm sorry," said Mr Macmaster, "but I can't do that. I will not hand over the keys to the safe unless I am instructed to do so by headquarters."

"You what?" said Evans. "I am ordering you to do so."

"I do not have the authority to do it without instruction from headquarters," said the postmaster, and walked away.

"We'll see about this!" said Evans. He stormed off down to the post office and informed Capt Stephen that he would have to get authority from Post Office headquarters before he could get the safe opened.

"Lance Corporal," said Captain Stephen, "telegraph to headquarters and get them to send a telegram to Mr Macmaster to hand over the keys. He won't give them to us – or rather to Col Evans, as he was the one to ask for them."

"Right, sir," said Jimmy. "I'll do that right away."

The Post Office staff were exercising in the prison yard. The weather was dreadful, wind and rain, but some were glad to be outside in the fresh air and the postmaster was taking the chance to speak to the overseers without worrying about being over heard.[1]

"I confess I am a little anxious about the situation," he said. "We could be held here indefinitely without any reason being given. The Defence of the Realm Act allows the military authority to do that."

"I know," said Hug. "I am not so worried for myself as for Leebie and the bairns."

"Surely they will at least question us today," said Willie Stout, "and then we should get some idea of what we are being accused of – or who they think is doing something wrong."

"I feel they are bound to do that at least," said Mr Macmaster. "As none of us seem to be aware of anything that we have done wrong, or anything that any others of the staff have done wrong – then they are bound to explain just what it is that they are accusing us of."

In another corner of the yard, several members of the staff were questioning the Post Office cleaner, William Spanswick.

"I tell you, they are bringing it this afternoon," said William.

"Are you sure?" said one of the younger members.

"What's being brought in?" asked George Manson.

"William's gramophone," said another.

"Hey, great," said George. "How many records have you got, William?"

"About four hundred," said William.

The rest gazed at him with great respect.

"That'll liven things up a bit," said one.

One of the senior postmen remarked that he had been out at the front of the prison.

"How did you do that?" asked someone.

"Well, I just wandered into a corridor and walked along to see where it led to and found myself out at the front!"

---

[1]   Letter from Mr Macmaster to George Manson dated 24th January 1957.

"Didn't you feel like nipping over to the brewery for a quick one?"

"Well, yes, I did," he said, "but then I remembered what John Morrison said and I thought it would get him into trouble so I didn't bother. But the thing is, when I was out there I saw some of the Territorials delivering some of the town's parcels. The ones that arrived with the steamer on Saturday night."

"Well, at least they're getting some of it done. Less for us when we get back."

"The trouble is," said the postman, "I had a half-mutchkin of whisky and when they arrested us all I had to put it somewhere so I stuck it in among the parcels, just to hide it. I thought we might be searched by the military."

"Well?"

"By now I bet the Terriers will have found it and polished it off!"

While they were in the yard, the convicted prisoners were cleaning their cells for them and when they were summoned back inside they found that the prisoners had done a splendid job. As they passed cigarettes through the traps in the doors to them by way of thanks they heard the warder coming upstairs again and several sets of footsteps following him. Wondering who was visiting now, they turned around and saw almost the whole complement of Lerwick's plumbers and gas-fitters heading into the corridor. The Prison Committee had made good its promise and the light fittings in the cells were being replaced as fast as possible.

Provost Stout hurried over to Braeside, Sheriff Menzies' house and knocked on the door. The maid let him in and the Sheriff came to meet him in the doorway.

"What's this I've been hearing?" asked Sheriff Menzies. "Is it true that the Post Office staff are in prison? Whatever for?"

"I have two of my sons in that prison," said Provost Stout. "I've asked them but they have no idea why they are in there. Not an inkling. They have not been told and they have not been questioned."

"Have you seen them?" asked the Sheriff.

"Yes," said Provost Stout. "I saw them yesterday when I took in their supper and this morning when I went in with breakfast for them."

"You're having to feed them?"

"Yes. Feed them and supply bedding and whatever they need. Well, the prison can't cope with numbers like that."

"You mean they are all in there?"

"Yes. The postmaster too."

"This is a disgrace. This is beyond everything," said the Sheriff.

"Can you do anything about it?" asked the provost.

*The telegraph to
Sheriff McLennan
about the
imprisonment of the
Post Office staff.*

*National Archives of
Scotland*

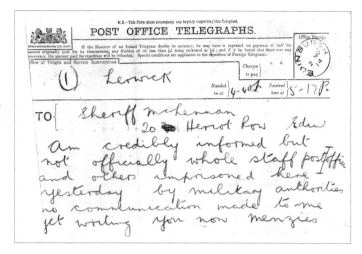

"Well, not really," said the Sheriff. "I know that sounds bad but I cannot do anything until I am notified officially and I have not been notified."

"Is there nothing at all you can do?"

"Perhaps something. I can telegraph Edinburgh and ask for advice. That is, if the telegraph links are working."

"Please try," said the provost.

A short time later there was another knock at the door and Sheriff Menzies found himself speaking to Mrs Macmaster. Her appeal to him was much the same and he regretted that he had to reply in similar terms. Until he was notified officially there was very little he could do. He decided, however, that he would try and get in touch with Sheriff McLennan in Edinburgh to lay the facts before him. He would send a telegram in the afternoon and would post a letter if need be at the same time in case the telegram was intercepted.

Jimmy Williamson went downstairs in search of Capt Stephen. He was carrying an envelope with the reply to his telegram, which had arrived from Post Office headquarters. On his way he met some of the Territorials who had been delivering parcels round the town.

"Hey, Jimmy," said one. "I found a very funny parcel in the bin."

"What?" said Jimmy. "No address, or what?"

"No. No address," said his friend. He winked.

"What was it? Come on!"

"Hmm. Well, it's disappeared now. We enjoyed it, I must say." He walked on, leaving Jimmy puzzled.

Jimmy found Capt Stephen and gave him the telegram. Capt Stephen said that he would deliver it personally.

He returned with Mr Macmaster in a short time and the postmaster opened the safe, handed over a supply of stamps and entered the necessary information in the books. He then asked if he could send a telegram acknowledging the instructions from headquarters and Capt Stephen took him to the telegraph room. Mr Macmaster filled in the form and handed it to Jimmy. Jimmy blinked a little when he looked at it but he gave Macmaster a wry smile and sat down to send it.

Macmaster returned to the prison under escort and Stephen turned to Jimmy and asked what it was that had made him smile.

"It was the address he gave," said Jimmy. "He sent it from Cell No. 1, H.M.Prison, Lerwick. That should stir them up a bit!"

Hug was pleased to see Leebie when she arrived with his dinner in a basket.

"I've packed it with cloth so I hope it will still be warm for you," she said.

"I'm glad you could come. I've been worried about you," said Hug. "How are you managing?"

"Oh! We're fine," said Leebie. "Jessie is with the bairns till I get back now. And the bairns are all fine. Jean is a bit worried and puzzled but she's not letting the rest worry."

"This is all a huge mistake," said Hug. "I don't know what the authorities think they're doing. We haven't seen anybody today to find out what is going on. That Col Evans was here this morning but only to deliver Hector Macrae and to demand that the postmaster give him the keys to the safe. He wouldn't do that, of course. He waited until he got a telegram from headquarters and then went down himself. He told us he sent a telegram back to headquarters and put Cell No. 1 on it as his address."

"Good for him! Maybe you'll see someone this afternoon. Surely!"

Hug took his dinner back upstairs and found it was still warm. He thought it was very good of Warder Morrison to let them see the people who came with their meals. It was some contact at least and it was good that Leebie had managed to come herself this time.

Soon after all the dinners had been delivered and eaten, there was a shout for William Spanswick and he disappeared downstairs. A hand-cart had arrived with his gramophone and records and he had to call for help to haul it all upstairs. Everyone helped to install it at the end of the corridor and soon William was asking for requests.

They were surprised that he could remember whether he had a particular tune or not, considering the size of the pile of records. Sometimes it took a little scuffling around before he could produce the goods but few were disappointed. The afternoon took on a festival air, even producing smiles in the passers-by outside.

"Well, they're not worried anyway," said one. "Sounds like a good party in there."

Sheriff Menzies sat down to write an urgent letter to Sheriff McLennan in Edinburgh.[2]

"I have now to report that I am credibly informed, though I have had no official communication from the military authorities, that they yesterday afternoon about 3 o'clock arrested the whole post office staff here with three exceptions who were afterwards taken into custody. Three mail drivers also are in custody. The men were taken to the prison here under a guard with fixed bayonets. They are still there as I write (4 pm) They are being supplied with food and comforts from their own homes. I have had calls from the Provost who has two sons arrested and from a solicitor acting for some of those arrested. I have also been approached by the wife of the Postmaster. In all cases I have had to say that I am totally ignorant of the matter and can do nothing until it is brought before me judicially. The Provost has been asked to call a public meeting, but I have influenced him against such a course as likely to lead to disturbance rather than do good. I understand however that as there are about 36 persons imprisoned unless their relatives and friends are given some information as to what is being done there is likely to be trouble. The post office is shut with a military guard with fixed bayonets at all points. It is to be open from 3–5 so I am off to see if I can wire to you or not."

In the wool shop, Mattie was standing looking white and scared.

"What's the matter?" asked one of the other assistants.

"That last customer!" said Mattie. "She said that all the Post Office men had been arrested because they were spies. And they were going to be shot and it served them right."

---

2   NAS, HH31/17.

"Her!" said another. "She doesn't know what she's talking about. She doesn't belong here anyway. She's a sooth moother.[3] What would she know about it?"

"She said she heard it from somebody at the fort," said Mattie.

"Rubbish. Nobody at the fort would speak to her anyway. Pay no heed to her!"

Jimmy Williamson was delighted to see Davie Tait when he arrived off the *Earl* that afternoon. He asked him if he would go straight away to the telegraph room while he himself made another attempt to organise the sorting office. There was very little time left before the boat left for Aberdeen with the mail for the south. He gave up any idea of trying to sort the letters before they went. It would be enough, he thought, if they could get them all stuffed into mailbags.

"Let Aberdeen sort them," he thought.

Peter Robertson and Jock Thomson appeared sometime after 4 o'clock.

"Hey, Jimmy," said Peter. "What's going on here? There's a queue outside in the rain waiting to post parcels and stuff and the sergeant on the door is only letting them in one by one! It's daft! They're getting soaked."

"Orders from on high I suppose," said Jimmy with a yawn. "Am I glad to see you two!"

Their arrival had coincided with that of Sheriff Menzies, who had come to see if there was any possibility of sending a telegram to Edinburgh.

"Can you guarantee that it will be sent as written and not interfered with?" asked the sheriff.

"It will be sent from here as you have written it," said Jimmy, "but I can't guarantee what will happen after that."

"I had better send a letter too," said Sheriff Menzies. He handed Jimmy the telegram form and sat down to write a hasty addition to his letter to Sheriff McLennan.

"Later.

"I have asked if a telegram to you would be sent through guaranteed not to be interfered with *en route*. I am told it will be sent from here as delivered to them, but they cannot answer for anything further. I have therefore handed in a telegram in following terms.[4]

"Sheriff McLennan, 20 Heriot Row, Edinburgh.

---

3   Most people arriving in Shetland by sea would enter Lerwick Harbour by the south mouth of Bressay Sound. Non-Shetlanders were therefore referred to as 'sooth moothers'.

4   NAS, HH31/17.

"Am credibly informed but not officially whole staff post office and others imprisoned here yesterday by military authorities. No communication made to me yet. Writing to you now

"Menzies."

He added: "This occurrence has naturally put everything else in the background. It is rumoured here that Kirkwall and Wick are similarly affected.

"Yrs truly

"Menzies."

After tea the lights in the cells were lit and immediately the cells and corridor were flooded with light. The contrast with the feeble glow of the day before was marked. Although the evening before could not have been said to be gloomy or dismal – not with the hilarity which had reigned throughout the corridors – the cheerful light from the new gas fittings brought a smile to their faces.

Sheriff McLennan received Sheriff Menzies' telegram just before 6 pm. He stared at it in amazement. "Why on earth would the military arrest the whole of the staff of the Lerwick Post Office?" he thought. "I wonder what Menzies thinks I can do about it?"

He decided that he had best consult the Lord Advocate and get his opinion.

Jimmy Williamson was battling to get the mail ready to deliver to the steamer to go south to Aberdeen. After trying to explain how to sort the letters to Territorials used to having letters delivered to them without questioning how it happened, he gave up and told them just to put them unsorted into the mailbags and then fasten them into the leather waterproof bags that they were required to use at present. Even that was taking an inordinate amount of time. He went in search of Capt Stephen.

"Sir, do you think you could delay the steamer for a little?" he asked.

"I'll do my best," said Capt Stephen. "If the agent can't do it, then I suppose nobody can. I'll go down to my office for a bit. Back in a little."

When he returned he told Jimmy that the steamer would wait for the mail, but to be as quick as possible. Jimmy drove his troops to increased activity.

At 6.30 pm the mails had been delivered and the steamer was ready to sail just half-an-hour late. At 6.30 pm a military escort marched Kenneth Mackenzie, protesting loudly, up to the jail after he had arrived in Lerwick. He joined the rest of the staff.

The postmaster was increasingly surprised and dismayed that there had still been no explanation forthcoming from the military authorities for their arrest. No-one had come to question them about anything. There was nothing but rumour and conjecture and imagination running riot.

The story of the woman in the wool shop was common knowledge although Mattie was not to blame for spreading it. It had grown to such an extent that it was now being reported that they were all to be shot and the firing squad had been picked for the job.

Mr Macmaster could discount most of the rumours but he was still very perturbed. He was not in the least worried about whether any of his staff were guilty of a misdemeanour – he knew perfectly well that none of them were – but what made him uneasy was the new act, the Defence of the Realm Act. He knew that they could be held in prison for an unspecified length of time without any charges being laid against them. There was no means of knowing how long they would be held. However he had decided in discussion with Hug and Willie Stout that there was nothing to be gained from alarming the men, most of whom seemed to be in a cheerful frame of mind, and indeed were inclined to treat the whole thing as a big joke. They would leave it like that, he thought, and turned his attention to reassuring his staff that he would do everything he could to get them all released as soon as possible.

The men were discussing what they should do to pass the time while they were in jail when the assistant warder announced the first of the families with the supper baskets. One by one they went down to fetch them. They noticed that the assistant warder was much more strict. He was inspecting all the baskets as they were handed over, lifting the lids on the pots and looking carefully at the contents.

"Did you see that?" said one of the men. "He was looking at all the food."

"Ah! But," said another, "he didn't look in the Thermos! Now, there's a thought!"

"No, you're right. He never took the top off the Thermos. Well, well."

"Yes," said another. "I think I know what to ask for next time!"

The new lights made reading possible in the cells when they had all settled down in bed. It was much quieter than it had been on the previous night.

Jimmy Williamson staggered home about midnight for a few hours sleep. He had been awake for at least forty hours and he knew that he would soon start making mistakes. Sleep was needed, if only for a few hours. Peter and Jock and Davie could carry on for the next few hours. He himself would be back before the mail started arriving again. It would get better. Relief staff were coming from Aberdeen with the steamer on Tuesday. He was not sure how many would be coming but Aberdeen had assured him that they would make sure the Post Office ran as usual. He doubted that, but some trained staff would help. He slept.

Most of the men in the cells were asleep and the new lights turned out, but the postmaster found it difficult to rest. He wondered if he should insist on seeing Evans and asking him to explain his conduct, but the little that he had seen of him did not lead him to believe that he would get any satisfactory answers. Perhaps it was better to leave Evans to come to them.

"Overcrowded" wrote Dr Yule firmly under Warder Morrison's daily statement.

CHAPTER 10

Tuesday, 3rd November, 1914

TUESDAY DAWNED with a hail of boots along the corridor. It was 6.30 am and William Spanswick had the bright idea of starting the day with a cheerful Harry Lauder song. Unfortunately he had chosen *Oh! It's Nice to Get Up in the Morning* and this had not proved popular with his jailmates; hence the stream of boots heading in his direction. He seized his precious gramophone and beat a hasty retreat into his cell. Most of the staff, however, once wakened by William's music, got up anyway to face the new day, to get washed, and to wait for their breakfasts.

Breakfast arrived and with it hurried snatches of news from outside. It seemed that the townspeople of Lerwick were becoming incensed at the treatment of the staff and the parade thrice daily of relatives and friends with food.

The postmaster was becoming increasingly concerned at the dearth of information about the detention of the staff and the puzzling lack of interrogation. He could not understand why none of them had been questioned. He concluded that the military must be making a search of the Post Office, but in this he was mistaken. The military were too busy trying to run the ordinary business of the Post Office with conspicuous lack of success.

The townspeople were amazed to see members of the Territorial Force trotting round Lerwick in a disorganised fashion delivering single letters here and there. One shopkeeper reported to his customers that no sooner had one letter been handed to him than another man would come with one more. Ten minutes later yet another 'postman' would arrive with a third. It took most of the morning and about twelve Territorials to deliver all his mail.

Yet another unfortunate found to his dismay, after a long trek through the town with one letter that he had the same long walk back with the next one. It dawned on another one that sorting through his pile and putting them in some kind of order might be of benefit; and so it might have been if he had not done his sorting on a flat wall. A fine wind blew the letters along the roadway and the resultant chase gave as much exercise as he wished.

After breakfast the staff were sent out to the exercise yard while the convicted men cleaned their cells. The weather had improved slightly and some of the men thought it would be a good idea to give the baby an airing. Its mother was pleased and so they took it in turns to carry it round the yard.

The unfortunate baby was in jail because its mother, one of the itinerant herring workers, had taken illegally accepted advance of wages from more than one employer against the promise to work for them at the herring gutting season and had thus incurred the penalty. The child was delighted with the extra attention it was getting, not least the change in scenery

In the corner of the yard, there was a heap of stones. It was part of the punishment of the convicted prisoners that they had to break up these stones for road mending. Hector MacRae, who came from Stornoway, went across and picked up a good-sized stone from the heap. He was a hefty fellow, almost six foot tall. He lifted the stone level with his shoulder and then threw it as far as he could. It flew from his hand and landed a good way away.

"Hey! Let me try that," said a voice and soon a good competition was in progress. Those who were not taking part stood and watched, applauding a good throw.

When they returned inside, William brought out his gramophone again and asked for requests. There was music too from some of the staff, who had asked for their instruments to be taken in to them. They accompanied William's records or struck up traditional Shetland airs. There was plenty of entertainment.

John Shewan was writing a postcard to his brother who was stationed with the cable guard at Mossbank.

"Cell 6, Downstairs, H.M.Prison. 3rd Nov. 14" he wrote. "Dear Brother, I am now in chokey. I don't know what for. There are four of us in a cell 10½ ft. x 8½ ft. Andrew Garriock, Alfred Hay, Bob Williamson & myself. Am having to be fed and clothed from home. Hope you are well. I am not so bad under the circumstances, from your loving Bro. John."

He addressed the postcard to Pte. Walter Shewan, Cable Guard, Mossbank, and gave it to the warder to send out.

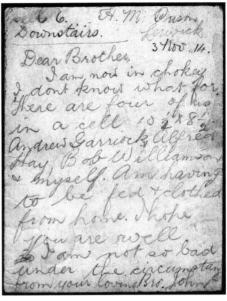

The postcard addressed to Pte Walter Shewan in Mossbank. (L Cpl Walter Shewan, Gordon Highlanders, was killed in action at Arras in April 1917, aged 25.)

At 10.15 am Sheriff Menzies went to the Post Office and sent another telegram to Sheriff McLennan, to Parliament House, Edinburgh.[1] He wrote: "Please say if my telegram of yesterday has reached you." He was becoming increasingly anxious about the situation, although he was not sure if there was anything he could do about it.

In the Post Office itself, Jimmy Williamson was battling away, trying to keep the situation under control. He had gone to speak to Capt Stephen and found him in the postmaster's office on the point of opening the official Post Office mail.

"I think you had better leave that, sir," he said. "You would probably not understand the instructions in it and it had better be left for the postmaster, when he gets out. Or for the head of the relief staff, when they get here."

"When are they arriving?" asked Stephen.

"They were to leave Aberdeen last might. Should arrive in Scalloway this afternoon or evening. Then they'll come here, I suppose."

"It was a rough night," said Stephen. "I won't have been a good trip."

---

1   NAS, HH31/17.

"Don't think so with this airt of wind," said Jimmy. "Meanwhile we struggle on."

"We do," said Capt Stephen, smiling.

The midday meal arrived in baskets and pails at the prison. With it arrived further rumours and gossip.

Mrs Macmaster looked anxiously at her husband.

"Have you still had no further explanation?" she asked. "Still no questions? Nothing?"

"Nothing at all," said the postmaster. "Nothing whatsoever. We have not seen Lt Col Evans or anybody else."

"Has Warder Morrison not been informed either?"

"No. He is as much in the dark as we are. All that he has been told is to give us every privilege as we are not under arrest – only being detained!"

"I can't see the difference if you are in jail," said Mrs Macmaster, sadly.

Although the press had not as yet got wind of the fact that the Admiralty had ordered the arrest of a large body of British civilians, rumours were spreading, in part due to Sheriff Menzies' frantic telegrams. There was a feeling of uneasiness among those in the know. Why, it was felt, were so many arrested – and the postmaster among them. It was not possible that they were all guilty of something. And of what precisely, in any case? Sheriff McLennan started a chain of questions which eventually reached the ears of the Admiralty itself, which promptly grew alarmed and started asking questions of its own, principally to the administration at Scapa Flow.

At 4.15 pm Sheriff Menzies received a reply to his letter and telegrams.

The telegram[2] read:

"3 Nov. 1914. Noon. Sheriff Menzies, Braeside, Lerwick.

"Telegrams of yesterday and today duly received. Consulted Lord Advocate on receipt of former. He advised we have no duty in matter at present. Deliberately abstained from wiring yesterday but wrote you. McLennan."

---

2   NAS, HH31/17 – handwritten copy.

"As I thought," he said. "There is nothing I can do until I am officially informed. But at least I have alerted Edinburgh to what is happening."

The Prison Committee paid another visit and inspected the new lights. Their visit had further benefits in that they announced that the lights could be left on until 10 pm in the cells. They were also to be allowed visitors the following day, Wednesday, between two and five in the afternoon.

"That's great," said George Manson. "I'll tell Mary when she comes up with my supper."

When relatives arrived with the evening meal, they were met with the good news that they could visit the prison the next day and spend up to three hours there.

"Well I never," said one. "I cannot believe all this. And there is such a change on this building; you would not credit it."

"That's right," added another. "It's all lit up – like a hotel or something. It looks cheery! Not dismal any more."

"And the noise coming out of it too, when you pass by. Music and laughing. Not like a prison at all!"

The assistant warder, the grumpy one, was on duty watching the baskets and pails being handed over. As before he lifted the lids to make sure there were no illicit foodstuffs being smuggled in. He nodded to the men to take their rations and with serious faces they carried their supplies upstairs.

"Wey, hey," said one, screwing the top off his Thermos and sniffing at the contents. "We've got away with it!"

Some of the cells became immediately more lively and feet began stamping merrily to fiddle tunes as the musicians got underway.

Later, Warder Morrison came round looking surprised but pleased.[3]

"I have some news for you," he said. "I have been informed by the officer in charge that some of you have been detained by mistake, if you please! Accordingly, these men are to be set free immediately. Apparently, the linesmen should not have been arrested, so that means that Andrew Garriock, John Mackay, John MacLennan, Hector Macrae and Kenneth MacKenzie are free to go now. There are also two

---

3   Prison record – NAS, HH31/17.

telegraphists who should not have been arrested and these are George Hood and John Weir. Gentlemen, follow me and I will see you discharged."

The remaining staff looked at each other in consternation.

"Does this mean that more of us will be let out tomorrow?" asked one.

"Why have the linesmen got out? Because they are not usually in the Post Office building?"

"It must be something to do with a letter right enough if the telegraphists are getting out."

"But it's only two of them. The rest of us are here still."

"They're not Shetlanders. Is that why?"

"Surely not."

Speculation was rife.

"I see that you now have forty prisoners," said Dr Yule to the warder. "Not really any improvement."

"Too little air space," he wrote under the warder's daily report.

Wednesday, 4th November, 1914

WEDNESDAY DAWNED with better weather. The wind had eased and there were fewer showers of rain. The inmates of Lerwick jail rose early as usual and went to wash. Their mood was cheerful as that day they had been promised visits from relatives and friends and they were looking forward to the chance of longer conversations. They would find out what was being said in the town. First, however, came breakfast and the men waited for their names to be called as relatives began to arrive with pots of porridge.

"Hey," said one of the men. "Look what I've got this morning. Boiled eggs. Great!"

He walked over to the door of one of the cells which still held convicted prisoners and tapped on it. The trap had been left open to let in air as Dr Yule had insisted. When a face appeared at the trap he passed two of his boiled eggs in.

"You can share that, boys," he said.

At 9 am Warder Morrison was told that another telegraphist was to be released.

"Who is it this time?" he asked.

"David Gunn," said the messenger. "He is to report for duty at the Post Office as soon as possible."

Morrison fetched David Gunn from the top corridor and told him he was to be released and should get to the Post Office as quickly as he could. David was at a loss to understand the reason for his release when the rest of his colleagues were still under lock and key. He wondered if it might be because of his temporary status at Lerwick. Like George Hood and John Weir, he had been sent to Lerwick because of the increase in telegraph traffic. He thought perhaps they had all been released because they were not part of the permanent staff here. He thanked Warder Morrison for the consideration he had shown to all of them and went away to work.

Jimmy Williamson was looking forward to getting some help in the Post Office. He was delighted that George Hood and John Weir had been released the night before and that David Gunn would be at work that day as well. That would make a real difference in the telegraph room. But even more important was the arrival of the relief staff from Aberdeen. They had arrived yesterday and should have found accommodation in Lerwick the night before.

"Message for you, Jimmy," said one of the telegraphists. He handed Jimmy a slip of paper. Jimmy read it and groaned.

"They're not coming in," he said.

"Who's not coming?"

"The relief staff. They're all sick after the passage from Aberdeen. Right enough, it was coarse weather, but …   oh, well! Carry on as usual, I suppose."

He stumped along the passage on his way to the sorting office.

Harriet Inkster was speaking to a friend outside the baker's shop. Harriet was walking out with George Hood and was overjoyed that he had been released. George came from Dundee originally but he and John Weir had been working in Edinburgh when they were sent north to help staff the telegraph room in Lerwick. The volume of telegraph traffic had increased dramatically after the Faeroese cable had been installed and the outbreak of war had added considerably to the load.

"I was never so surprised in my life," said Harriet. "It was fairly late before they let him out but we were all so pleased to see him. Thank goodness."

"I am really pleased for you," said her friend. "Does he know when the rest will get out?"

"No, he doesn't know," said Harriet. "You know, I've been so worried. You know, George is dark – his complexion is dark."

"So?"

"Well, I really thought that if they thought there was a spy, they would think it was George because he's so dark. Like a foreigner."

"Oh, surely they wouldn't! Anyway, they don't think that! They've let him out. Where is he now?"

"Back at work. He thinks that that is why they let him out. So he could go back to work. They're in a rare old muddle there, I think."

The better weather tempted the prisoners to stay out a little longer in the exercise yard. One of them had fetched the baby and they took it on turns to walk round with it. The baby was delighted with the fresh air and gurgled away happily.

A trial of strength was in progress again in the corner of the yard with the stones. Cries of "Heave it!" and "Don't drop it over your shoulder!" echoed between the walls. The wind began to rise a little again and a spattering of rain drove them inside. They waited eagerly for their dinner to arrive and the longed-for visitors.

Although the Lord Advocate had told Sheriff McLennan that there was nothing that he could usefully do at present, he was determined to find out what, if anything, was being done by other agencies and accordingly he went to see the Secretary to the GPO in Edinburgh, Mr Kirkwood. They discussed the affair at some length and Sheriff McLennan learned that the Post Office was sending a surveyor north to Shetland to see what the situation was and to find out what was happening to the Lerwick Post Office.[1]

The Post Office was extremely concerned about it. It seemed that the military authority in Shetland, who had slung the whole staff in jail, had appointed a junior member of staff with only two years' experience to run the place with the help of the local Territorial Force. A Territorial captain was in overall charge but with none of these men with any Post Office training, except one, Kirkwood considered it would be a shambles.

"Relief staff are being sent from Aberdeen to help but it will still not be enough," he said. "This whole situation is ridiculous. Slinging the whole lot in jail like that! And as far as I can make out nobody has any idea as to why they are in there or how long they are going to keep them in."

"Will you let me know if there is anything that we can do about it?" asked McLennan.

"Yes, certainly," said Kirkwood. "I should know a little more once Dunlop, the surveyor, reaches Lerwick."

---

1   Information on this from handwritten letter from Sir J.M. Dodds – NAS, HH31/17.

At a quarter to one Warder King returned to the Lerwick prison.[2]

"Am I glad to see you," said Morrison. "I am run off my feet here. The Post Office staff have been allowed visits from family and friends this afternoon and they will all be arriving shortly. Thank goodness you're here to help."

The wind was still rising from the north-east when family and friends began to arrive for the promised visit. They stood shivering in a queue, awaiting their turn to be let in. The grumpy warder was on duty and eyed them morosely. He read out a long selection of prison rules to them and ended by giving them a stern warning about the dangers of slipping notes to the inmates between two slices of bread and butter. As the majority of those waiting had never thought of that idea they stared at him in amazement.[3]

Finally they were allowed inside, out of the biting wind. They wait had been worth it though, they all considered. It was a relief to be able to see for themselves that the prisoners were all right and great to be able to talk to them for a while. The chatter of voices grew louder.

"Are you all right, Mary?" asked George Manson.

"I'm fine," said Mary. "Do you know how long you are going to be here yet?"

"No. We still have no idea. We haven't seen anyone and not one of us has been questioned at all about anything. Not asked one question. Nothing."

"I have heard from a friend of mine in Kirkwall," said Mrs Macmaster to her husband. "She says that there are German prisoners of war in Kirkwall and they are being kept in the town hall, if you please, and are being fed from a hotel!"

"Goodness me!" said the postmaster.

"They can treat the enemy like that, but up here our own men who are guilty of nothing are being treated like common criminals. I am furious."

"There is really nothing we can do. We will just have to wait and see what Evans does. At least some of our men got out last night. Maybe some more will get out soon."

"I am going to see the Provost again and Sheriff Menzies. There must be something we can do. Write a letter or something."

"At least we are being treated in here with every courtesy that Mr Morrison can possibly give us. He has been very good. It could have been so much worse. He is so concerned about our health always. Leaves the traps open at night and we are only in our cells to sleep. Dr Yule is round every day. We are as well looked after as Warder Morrison can manage."

---

2   Warder King's return – from official report by D. Crombie – NAS, HH31/17.
3   Report in the *Orcadian*, 5th November, 1914.

"Well, that is something to be thankful for," said Mrs Macmaster

The visits were supposed to last only ten minutes for each man but the ten minutes seemed to be fairly elastic. Finally however the last visitor departed and the jail settled down to its usual routine.

"Let's have a whist drive tonight," said a voice.

"Hey! Great idea!" said another. "Do we have enough cards?"

It seemed that they did. Enough of them had asked family and friends to bring in playing cards and it was soon organised.

"Cigarettes for prizes!" said another voice.

The postmaster was enjoying the whist drive enormously. The standard of play was high and he was glad to concentrate on something other than the situation that they found themselves in.

"Did you go to the prison today?" asked Mattie.

"Yes. I did go and I saw Jeemsie," said Leebie. "We had a while together but he couldn't tell me anything at all."

"They still haven't been told why they're in there?"

"No. They haven't been told anything and nobody has come in to question them about anything either. I know Jeemsie is worried. He said he wasn't but I know. They could be kept in there for a long time under this new law."

Mattie looked at Leebie. She was very worried about her. She wasn't going to mention it but Leebie's hair had turned white almost overnight since the men had been arrested and she was looking tired and ill. The bairns were too young to understand properly, thought Mattie. That was something to be grateful for at least. Although it seemed to her that Jean understood more than she was admitting.

In his log book as usual Warder Morrison made a note of the cells occupied and the number of men in each.[4]

"10 cells with 3 Post Office officials each   30

"1 cell with 2   do.   do.   2"

Under the last entry he added a curious little note:

"As there is only 2 in this cell leave light in cell and place under observation."

On the warder's log book Dr Yule wrote firmly "Too little air space".

---

4   Copy of Prison Report – NAS, HH31/17.

The Under Secretary for Scotland, Sir James Dodds, was at the New Club in Edinburgh when, shortly before midnight, Sheriff McLennan came looking for him.

"Have you heard about the Lerwick Post Office staff?" asked Sheriff McLennan.

"No," said Sir James. "I've heard nothing. What has happened?"

"They've all been arrested," said Sheriff McLennan. "For spying, supposedly."

"What? All of them?"

"Every last one. Telegram boys too, I think. Postmen, telegraphists, the lot."

"Are they all accused of spying? Seems a bit wholesale."

"Nobody seems to know *what* they are accused of," said Sheriff McLennan. "I heard of it from Menzies. Some of the family members got in touch with him and he telegraphed to ask my advice. But there is really nothing we can do at present."

"There have been no reports in the newspapers."

"No, but I don't expect it will be very long until they get hold of it. I have been to see Kirkwood, the secretary for the GPO, but he does not know anything either. He is sending a surveyor up to Lerwick so he may know more then."

"Who is responsible for this?" asked Sir James.

"I really don't know if it is the Army or the Navy," replied McLennan. "It seems to have been a Col Evans who made the arrest. He must be in charge there in some capacity."

"Thank you for telling me. Are these papers connected with it?"

"Yes. This is the correspondence from Menzies – letters and telegrams. Thought you should see it all."

"I had better warn Westminster. Someone is bound to have contacted Wason I imagine. After all he is the MP for there. He is sure to ask questions and it will be better if they have some knowledge of what is happening first. I will write straight away."

He sat down at a desk and drew some paper towards him.[5]

"4th Nov. 1914. Midnight.

My Dear Lamb,

Enc. Papers have just been given me by Sheriff McLellan. It is a curious business suggestive of Zabern methods. I suppose there is a suspicion of leakage of information but the proceedings are somewhat wholesale. I shd. think you will have a visit from Wason soon. McLellan was anxious to say something so I told him he might say he had given me the papers.

---

5   Letter from Dodds to Secretary for Scotland – NAS, HH31/17.

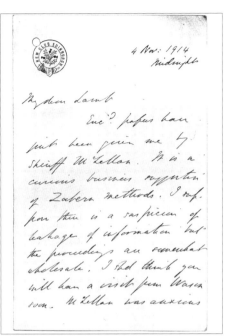

"He had seen Kirkwood the G.P.O. secretary here: also the Lord Advocate who thought it was not his business. Whether it is or is not only time will shew: I may see Kirkwood or the military tomorrow but meanwhile I send the papers on. You may know all about it.

"It is not clear whether it is the Army or Navy which has acted. McLennan thinks probably a Colonel Evans of Marines.

Yours ever,

J.M.Dodds."

The letter from Dodds to Lamb about the 'curious business'.

National Archives of Scotland

CHAPTER 12

Thursday, 5th November, 1914

ON THURSDAY MORNING the *Aberdeen Free Press* carried a headline 'LERWICK POST OFFICE' and underneath that 'ARREST OF THE STAFF' in smaller capitals.[5]

"Writing on Monday", it said, "a Shetland correspondent says:-
Great excitement was caused in Lerwick on Sunday afternoon by the arrest of most of the Post Office staff by a strong contingent of armed R.N.R. men and their conveyance to the County Buildings, where they have since been confined. Up to Monday afternoon the officials (said to number between 30 and 40) were still under confinement, and so far as known no special charge has been made against them. Several rumours are current – one that some of the telegraphic instruments had been tampered with; another that information had leaked out through members of the staff, &c.; but these are probably mere surmises, as great reticence is being maintained by the authorities. Meantime, representatives of the R.N.R. and local Territorials are in charge of the Post Office, the deliveries today (Monday) having been carried out by Territorials. Intimation was made in the morning that the office would only be open for one hour in the forenoon and three hours in the afternoon, and that only Government service telegrams would be accepted for transmission. Considerable indignation is being expressed at the inconvenience to the general public. Officials have visited and searched the homes of the men and boys arrested, including not only the telegraphists and clerical staff, but also the linesmen, postmen, and messengers. It is

---

I   *Aberdeen Free Press*, 5th November, 1914 (Further report in *Evening Dispatch*, Edinburgh – 5th Nov.)

reported that, following the arrest of the officials, their relatives had orders sent to them to send supplies of food and bedding to them; and it is pointed out that, even if they had been prisoners of war, they would have been provided for by the authorities who arrested them. Situated as they are, almost two hundred miles by sea from Aberdeen, Shetland business men have come to depend more on the telegraph service than men on the mainland, who receive several mails a day, and the curtailment of the telegraph service, even if it be only temporary, will be very severely felt by the community.

"This message has been submitted to the Press Bureau, which does not object to the publication, and takes no responsibility for the correctness of the statement."

News of the affair had reached the national press. Other papers were quick to pick it up.

Jimmy Williamson and his colleagues were more than delighted to see the relief staff come through the door. They welcomed them with open arms and conducted them round the building.

The overseer who had been sent with them to act as relief postmaster took one horrified look at everything and turned to Capt Stephen.

"We can't possibly sort this out by ourselves," he said. "We don't have enough knowledge of how this Post Office is run and there will be a huge backlog of details to cope with. I really need to have Postmaster Macmaster here to help us."

"I don't know what Colonel Evans will say to that," replied Capt Stephen. "If you want to approach him, you will find him at Fort Charlotte."

The overseer found his way there and demanded to see Lt Col Evans. He put his case for help forcibly and told Evans that no good would be served by disrupting the service further. The relief staff were trained men but they had no knowledge of the workings of the Lerwick Post Office and needed the help of the men who worked there.

"Oh, very well," said Evans. "Ask Warder Morrison to let the postmaster and one other man go down to the Post Office to help you. I will send an escort for them as it is not possible to let them out without one while they are still under detention."

Morrison agreed immediately to send for the postmaster and the overseer put his request to him.[2]

"We cannot possibly get things under control down there without your help," he said. He was quite unprepared for Mr Macmaster's reply.

"Certainly not," he said. "I have no intention of returning there until I have been properly released from prison along with *all* of my staff. We are none of us guilty of anything. If I were to go down and help you it would look as though I was admitting that we were at fault. And we are not. I will not go."

"But we cannot manage without you," said the overseer in consternation. "If you won't come, can I request help from one of your staff."

"You can ask," said Mr Macmaster. "I do not know what they will say. But you can ask, if you want."

The postmaster went back upstairs and sought out Hug Tait.

"I've just been asked, by one of the relief staff, to go down and help them sort out the mess in the Post Office. I have refused. He will probably ask you next."

"I will not be going either," said Hug.

"Well," said Macmaster, "I would be better pleased if you did go. I cannot go obviously. It would look like an admission of guilt of some kind. But if you don't go we won't have a Post Office to go back to when all this is over. If you go now with them, then perhaps the muddle will not be too bad. If we delay it will just get worse and worse."

"Hmm!" said Hug. "Well, all right. If you want me to go, then I will – under protest."

"Thanks!"

The overseer from Aberdeen heaved a sigh of relief when Hug agreed to go with him.

"I'm glad you've agreed," he said. "The whole thing is at sixes and sevens down there. We need someone who knows the ropes. If you had refused I was going to go back to Colonel Evans and get him to order one of you down."

"I will need another man," said Hug, "to help."

"Take whoever you want," said the overseer. "I will make sure that Evans knows."

---

2   Details of members of the staff going down to help:
    (a)   *Orcadian* report of 5th December, 1914.
    (b)   "The Lerwick Post Office Mystery" by Margaret Henderson in *The Scots Magazine*, November 1976.
    (c)   Account told to me by my mother, Jean.

Hug reported to the postmaster and asked one of the men to go down with him. When they got outside they found an armed escort waiting for them and in this fashion they accomplished the return march to the Post Office.

"Look at that!" said a voice in the street. "There's Hug still being marched around. It's just not good enough." He dived into the grocer's shop, grabbed a rotten apple and rushed out again.

"Take that!" he shouted and hurled the apple at the nearest man. The fact that the escort was composed for the most of local Shetland volunteers did not deter him. The armed guard faced a barrage of missiles as they marched along.

In the shelter of the post office the escort mopped its collective brow and sat down in a corner to wait until dinnertime.

Sir James Dodds had not been idle. He had spoken to Kirkwood and had requested immediate information from the Prison Commission for Scotland. He felt very uneasy about the whole affair. Certainly, he thought, Isles MP Cathcart Wason would make a lot of noise about it and that would cause a great deal of embarrassment for the Government. He considered it more than likely that Wason would be entirely justified in making a loud noise. There was something extremely suspicious about the way that it had been handled. The military authority in Shetland could not have thought that the whole of the staff were involved in spying, surely, so why had they not been interrogated first before this wholesale incarceration.

Furthermore, since the staff had been in prison since Sunday and this was now Thursday, it should have been possible to eliminate most of them from their enquiries. More and more he felt the comparison with Zabern was justified. Things were not done in that way in Britain, but using these 'Zabern methods' could result in a similar outcome; alienation of the local population. There would of course be no rioting, not in wartime, but it was essential to keep the locals 'onside' as it were.

He decided that he would have to see someone from the military, firstly for information, and secondly to put forward the political point of view, before the affair escalated out of hand.

It had been agreed that, at dinnertime, 1 pm, Hug Tait and the man assisting him could go home to eat instead of returning to the prison and someone having to deliver their dinner there. It had been decreed, however, that an armed escort had to be sent with

The daunting sight that would have greeted the prisoners. One of the original cell doors from Lerwick Police Station, now in the possession of Shetland Museum and Archives, after recent renovations.

Photo: Shetland Museum and Archives Photo Library

them and accordingly, at 1 pm, the escort rose from its seats, divided in two and set off again through the street. The men looked warily round them but the onslaught of the morning was not repeated and Hug reached 12 Commercial Street in a very short time.

Leebie was pleased and thankful to see him, but annoyed that he had to go back to jail after work.

"It's good that they let you come home for your dinner, though," she said. "I have it ready. Come in the kitchen."

"Listen, Mr Tait," said one of the escort. "I know we're supposed to watch you the whole time, but, well, so long as we're in the house, we can be watching you. Is there somewhere else we could sit?"

"Just go in the parlour," said Leebie. "I'll bring you a cup of tea."

"That was good of them," she said, returning to the kitchen.

"It's not their fault," said Hug. "They just have to do what they're told. Don't say that they were in the other room, will you?"

"No, of course I won't," said Leebie. "It's just so good to be able to talk to you without anyone else listening. Is there any news yet about when you are getting out?"

"No," said Hug with a sigh. "No news. We haven't seen anyone at all. Evans has not spoken to any of the men. Mr Macmaster has still not found out anything. We don't know why we are in there."

"Surely they won't keep you much longer?"

"They can keep us as long as they like under the new act – the Defence of the Realm Act. It's no use me telling you otherwise."

"Everybody you speak to is furious. None of them liked that Evans before but now they're blaming him for this and hating him worse than ever."

"Well," said Hug. "He's not particularly likeable, I must confess, but in this case he's just acting under orders from the Admiralty. They're the ones to blame."

It was time to return to the Post Office. The RNR men of the escort had been glad of the cup of tea and biscuits and thanked Leebie. Hug clapped his hat on his head, hugged Leebie and went out into the street again. He was more worried than ever. Leebie's hair had turned white with the worry and he did not know how her health would stand up to the stress if they were kept in much longer.

Back at the Post Office the amount of work that had to be done distracted his thoughts from the problem but anxiety gnawed away at the back of his mind continually.

Mr Dunlop, the Post Office surveyor who had been sent by headquarters in Edinburgh, arrived in Lerwick with his assistant. His instructions were to find out the conditions under which the Lerwick staff were being held. He approached Warder Morrison and asked if he could see the postmaster in his cell. Morrison replied that he would have to ask the Prison Commissioners for Scotland. He would telegraph them immediately, he said, and let Mr Dunlop know the result.

Sir James Dodds' request for information was being answered by James Devon of the Prison Commission for Scotland.[3] He had gathered as much information as he could. He considered that the prison authorities had done as much as they were capable of and were not to blame for the current situation. Mr Devon's opinion was that the blame lay with the Officer Commanding HM Forces in Shetland. He replied at some length to the Under Secretary for Scotland.

> Prison Commission for Scotland
> Edinburgh.5th November 1914.
> Sir,
> The Prison Commissioners have the honour to report that on the morning of the 2nd instant they received a telegram from the Warder in charge of Lerwick Prison, stating that 36 members of the Post Office staff and 2 mail drivers had been admitted to prison on the afternoon of Sunday, 1st instant, by Order of the Officer Commanding H.M. Forces in Shetland. (The Commissioners are informed that the Shetland Isles are under the Admiralty). The number was subsequently increased to 40, but 8 of these have since been liberated, leaving 32 still in prison. The Officer Commanding informed the warder in charge of the Prison that he is acting on confidential Admiralty instructions. The Commissioners understand that the officials arrested include the whole Post Office staff in Lerwick from the Postmaster downwards. As there are only 15 cells in the prison, and as there are six convicted male and one convicted female prisoners in confinement in addition to the Post Office officials (who now occupy 11 cells) the Warder in charge at the request of the Commissioners reported to the Officer Commanding the insufficient accommodation in the prison for all these officials, and possible danger to their health, and suggested their removal

---

3   Letter dated 5th November 1914 from J. Devon to Sir J.M. Dodds – NAS, HH31/17.

elsewhere. In reply the Officer Commanding stated that he has no other place to which he could transfer them, and that he does not know how long they are to be detained, his orders being to keep them under arrest pending investigation.

The Post Office Authorities at the Head Office in Edinburgh have protested against their officers being thus overcrowded in prison, but, as the Commissioners did not feel free to instruct the Warder in charge to refuse the Officer Commanding the use of the prison, they, having informed him of the limited accommodation in the prison, do not consider themselves responsible for the use to which he instructs it to be put, and think that any complaint by the Post Office Authorities should be addressed to the Naval Authorities and not to the Commissioners. The Commissioners have today received by telegram from the Warder in charge a request that a Post Office Surveyor from Edinburgh should be allowed to see the Postmaster in his prison cell in order that the Surveyor may see the conditions under which the Post Office staff has been accommodated, and the Commissioners have telegraphed to the Warder in charge approving of the surveyor seeing the cells and conditions, if authorised by his chief (the Secretary, General Post Office, Edinburgh) to do so, but that no interview should take place in cells. Inspector Mr Crombie will leave Edinburgh today for Lerwick in order that, in consultation with the Officer Commanding the Troops, he may make the best arrangements possible in the public interest.

It may be mentioned that the Post Office officials are being allowed to smoke and to have musical instruments – privileges never granted to ordinary prisoners, and that every effort is being made to make them as comfortable as possible in the circumstances. Bedding, clothing, and food are being supplied to them by their friends.

A copy of the Order committing them to prison is attached.

I have the honour to be, Sir,

Your most obedient Servant,

Jas. Devon.

"You can interview Mr Macmaster," said Warder Morrison, "but not in his cell. Perhaps you could speak to him at the Post Office."[4]

"Well, certainly," said Mr Dunlop. "That would be fine. Can I take it that you will let him out to come down there?"

---

4   Confirmed in letter from Mr Macmaster to George Manson, dated 24th January, 1957.

"Yes, of course," said the warder, "but I am afraid that the officer in charge will insist on sending an armed escort with him."

"Well, we can put up with that if we have to," said the Surveyor.

Shortly afterwards, the postmaster, with the inevitable escort, arrived outside the Post Office and followed Mr Dunlop into his own erstwhile office. There was no shortage of topics of conversation.

Prisons inspector Mr D Crombie left Edinburgh bound for Lerwick. His official instructions were to ascertain that the treatment of the Post Office staff had been proper and according to regulations, and to try to discover why the Officer Commanding HM Forces in Shetland had seen fit to put the staff in jail, and had not confined them in his headquarters, or the Town Hall as being more fitting. His unofficial instructions were 'to find out what that blithering idiot thinks he's doing!'

At Westminster Cathcart Wason, MP for Orkney and Shetland, sought out the Secretary for Scotland, Thomas McKinnon Wood, and demanded to know what he was doing about the Lerwick Post Office affair. Fortunately for Wood, he had been briefed by a member of his staff.

"Terrible business that," he said. "Don't understand what they mean by arresting the whole staff. Surely they don't think they are all guilty?"

"None of them are guilty," said Wason. "Somebody has blundered here."

"Well, you know," said the Secretary for Scotland, "there must be some doubt about that. They can't have arrested them for nothing. Must be some reason."

"There seems to be no reason attached to it."

"Well, we can make some representations to the Admiralty about it anyway," said the Secretary. "I feel that they have been a trifle high-handed over this."

"I am going to see someone from the Admiralty now," said Wason. "I don't intend to let this rest."

At the Admiralty also the Lerwick Post Office affair was under discussion. Questions were being asked. Awkward questions. The fact that the newspapers were reporting the incident was making discussions more urgent and information was being demanded from Vice-Admiral Sir Stanley Colville, the officer responsible at Scapa Flow.

No-one could understand the reason for the need to imprison the entire staff. The Admiralty had been alerted to the fact that the Vice-Admiral thought the mail between Orkney and Shetland was being tampered with and indeed some of the suspected mail had been sent to the Admiralty for examination. So far no signs of tampering had been found. The cover of the letter that had been forwarded to them did not look as though it had been interfered with. They would need to be looked at again, of course, to make sure, but it seemed like a storm in a teacup.

If there was any suspicion of tampering with the mail, then of course the Post Office staff should be interrogated but to arrest the whole staff and sling them in jail was going too far, especially now the press had got wind of it.

When Wason arrived at the Admiralty they had still not come to any definite conclusions on the subject. Wason emphasised the damage that was being done to relations between the population of Shetland and the military authorities there. He had conclusive evidence that none of the staff had been told why they had been arrested or had even been interrogated at all. They were languishing in prison with no effort being made to resolve the situation.

The staff member he was speaking to made little response beyond saying that they were looking into the affair.

The new Lerwick Post Office.

Photo: J Manson, Shetland Museum and Archives Photo Library

"I want something done immediately," said Wason. "I will be tabling a question in the Commons."

When Wason had gone, discussion of the affair became if possible more urgent and filtered rapidly up through the hierarchy. A decision had to be made.

Hug returned to the jail after work to find that the inmates had arranged a smoking concert for that evening and everyone was required to do a turn. As he hadn't got his double bass he wasn't sure what he could contribute. Perhaps he could team up with someone to sing a song or something.

The concert began in fine style with some traditional fiddle tunes and soon everyone's feet were tapping in time to the rhythm.

"Grand stuff, boys!" shouted Warder Morrison from his seat at the back.

"Come on, John," said a voice. "Your turn!"

John Arthur got to his feet and gave a spirited rendering of the song *Molly O'Morgan and Her Little Organ*. This was greeted with loud applause.

Act followed act. William Thomson recited *Auld Mansie's Crö* by Basil R. Anderson.

"Oot-ower apon a weel-kent hill," he began. "Whase waters rise ta grinnd a mill, Auld Mansie's biggit him a crö…."

Then George Manson took the floor and soon had the whole gathering holding their sides with laughter at his rendering of a German gentleman on the telephone.

"… I vant you to send a man to mend … no, no, not two men, one man, de carpenter, de man vot hits de nail mit de hammer …"

So loud was the laughter that it echoed through the street outside, startling passers-by. Such hilarity coming from the prison was unprecedented.

Time flew by and Hug realised with relief that there would not be time for him to contribute. The Postmaster rose and thanked all the participants and in good humour the inmates went to bed.

"Too little air space" wrote Dr Yule in the Warder's log.

CHAPTER 13

Friday, 6th November, 1914

THE PRISONERS woke to the now familiar routine. After visiting the washroom there was the usual wait until breakfasts began to arrive and news filtered from the outside world. Now that the Post Office telegraph room was adequately staffed once more the war news was being received again and printed by the local papers each day.

"It seems that we're in the south papers," said a voice. " 'Lerwick Post Office staff arrested', it says. There's been no mention in the local papers."

"I expect they'll have been told to keep quiet," said another. "What else does it say in the south paper?"

"I don't know. I just heard that bit. Nothing else."

Mr Macmaster was increasingly worried. There was no sign of any activity on the part of the military to question the staff or to let them know what they were being accused of. He wondered how long it would be before they were given any information. He worried incessantly about how the men's families would cope with no wages being paid to the men. The uncertainty of it all was worse than anything else. Warder Morrison was as much in the dark as they were. He was being given no information either.

"I've asked if I can have another man with me today," said Hug. "There's a lot of muddle to sort out down there. Captain Stephen and Jimmy have done their best but you can imagine what it's like."

"That's fine," said the postmaster. "The Aberdeen staff will be getting used to it too. That should help."

"Yes. Well," said Hug, "they are doing their best as well. It's just so busy."

Hug collected his two helpers and the escort and marched down to the Post Office. There were comments, mutterings and grumbles from all sides but the escort was relieved to see no hail of rotten fruit and vegetables heading in their direction. They reached the Post Office unsplattered.

The relative calm in the prison was not echoed in the corridors of the Admiralty in London.[1] None of the questions being asked seemed to have a satisfactory answer. The Admiralty had had the cover of the suspicious letter examined carefully by the Post Office Investigative Branch and they had found no evidence of tampering. The officials in the Admiralty were beginning to think that any further letters that were sent to them would prove just as enigmatic.

"I feel that they have become infected with some kind of 'spy-fever'," said one official. "There has been so much talk in the papers, most of it unfounded. They are probably seeing spies where none exists."

"Admiral Sir George Warrender sent a signal to the Fleet at the beginning of the War about a possible German base in Shetland," said another. "It seems that there was some doubt about the allegiance to Britain of the Shetlanders."

The other stared at him.

"I can't feel that there is any substance in that," he said. "There are countless numbers of Shetlanders in the Royal Navy."

"The First Lord himself seemed to think there was some doubt about it. He felt that the Territorials should be strengthened to insure that the population stayed on the right side as it were. German influence before the war or something."

"I don't believe it. And neither does Wason obviously. He is going to make a lot of trouble over this if we don't do something. And I think he will be justified. It was a crass mistake to arrest the whole lot, and as far as I can see whoever is in charge up there is making no push to find out who is guilty – if anyone is."

"The whole affair has been bungled. If the locals were loyal before, this is enough to alienate them altogether. Better get it settled quick."

It was decided eventually that the only option was to send a telegram to the Vice-Admiral, Sir Stanley Colville, at Scapa Flow telling him to release all of the Lerwick Post Office staff unless he had found proof that any of them were guilty. The telegram was duly sent.

"Let's hope that satisfies Wason and the Secretary for Scotland," said a naval secretary, Grant by name. "We can expect more visits from them in the near future, I should think."

---

1   Memo to Postmaster General initialled R.M., dated 26th February, 1915 – The British Postal Museum & Archive.

By the time the telegram reached the Vice-Admiral, it was afternoon. He prepared a dispatch for Lerwick, to be taken north by HMS *Sappho*, which was stationed at Scapa Flow. He was considerably annoyed about the whole incident. He had felt certain that the mail was being tampered with and Lerwick was the only place that could have happened. He had ordered that the staff be detained and questioned. That was the sensible thing to do. But someone had exceeded orders and slammed the whole lot in jail. Something like that was sure to cause an uproar, and so it had been. Now he was having to order that they were all released and apparently no-one had thought to question them when they *were* in jail. It was ludicrous. There was no possibility now of finding the guilty ones. If any of them were guilty. Obviously, from the contents of the telegram, the Admiralty did not consider that there was any charge to answer. No evidence of any tampering with the mail, they said. The Vice-Admiral wondered if any of them had even looked at it.

He handed the dispatch to the commander of HMS *Sappho* with instructions to see that it was acted upon immediately he reached Lerwick.

Mrs Macmaster was again anxiously asking if there had been any developments when she delivered the postmaster's supper.

"And Lt Col Evans has still not questioned any of you?"

"We've never seen him," said Mr Macmaster. "We've never seen any of the military. And I don't think Warder Morrison has either. He would have told us. The only contact he has had with them is to ask them if I could go down to the Post Office to speak to the surveyor, Mr Dunlop."

"It is all very worrying. I have been to see as many of the wives of the staff as I can manage. I am quite concerned for them. They are trying to put a cheerful face on it, but there is nothing cheerful about it. They are all afraid, as I am."

"Now," said the postmaster. "There is absolutely nothing to be afraid of. None of us are guilty and they will soon find that out. This is Britain, you know. There is such a thing as justice here."

"Huh!" said Mrs Macmaster. "If there was such a thing as justice here, none of you would be here at all."

"Don't worry. It will be all right. You'll see."

"I hope so. I will keep believing that." Mrs Macmaster sighed. "Well, I had better go. And by the way," she said, "I gave Mr Morrison the parcel I got for you. I collected it on my way here. The shop had it ready for me."

"Splendid," said the postmaster. "We can present it tonight."

The Prisons Inspector went in search of Evans. He found him at Fort Charlotte and asked him if he would answer some questions about the arrest of the Post Office staff.[2]

"Certainly," said Evans. "Go ahead!"

"Can you tell me the reason for the arrest of the staff?" asked Mr Crombie.

"I was acting on confidential instructions when I arrested the staff," said Evans. "Instructions from the Vice-Admiral of the Orkneys and Shetland."

"Why did you send them to the Lerwick prison?" asked Crombie.

"I sent them there as it was the only suitable place for their proper and safe custody."

"Well, the Prison Service is always keen to assist other government departments, but in this case it seems to me that they might well have been detained in the fort, or the Territorial drill hall, or the town hall – or a church or some other hall. There should surely be lots of alternatives to sending men of this kind to a common prison. They could have been spared that indignity."

"I did not consider that the sanitary arrangements and other things would have been adequate. And the fort was inconvenient – it would have interrupted the work of the military."

"Well," said Mr Crombie, "it does not seem to me that the procedure has been quite in the terms of the Act, regulation number 13, second paragraph."

"Well, as to that," replied Evans, "I do not feel I can express any view on that point."

Later in the evening Mr Macmaster called all the staff together.

"It is my very pleasant duty," he said, "to present this wedding gift on behalf of you all to George Manson. I hope it will give him and his wife long years of pleasure."

He handed the parcel to George who thanked them all profusely and proceeded to open it.

"Oh, how lovely," he said, holding up the clock for everyone to see. "Mary will love this. Many thanks, all of you. We'll treasure it."

"Too little air space" wrote Dr Yule stubbornly in the warder's log.

---

2   Confidential report by D. Crombie, dated 9th November, 1914 – NAS, HH31/17.

CHAPTER 14

Saturday, 7ᵗʰ November, 1914

HMS *SAPPHO* steamed into Lerwick harbour and the Commander lost no time in seeking out Cdr Startin on HMS *Shemara*.

"Dispatch for you," he said. "Instructions from the Vice-Admiral."

Startin opened the dispatch and read it.

"Well," he said. "I am not altogether surprised. I thought the whole thing mad from the start, but orders are orders."

"I suppose you will be setting them all free as soon as possible."

"Well, yes, certainly. This indicates that none of them are guilty anyway."

Startin went to find Evans.

"I do not understand this at all," said Evans. "I have had no instructions about questioning these men, no information except that it was suspected that mail had been tampered with. And now I have to set them free without questioning. It seems very irregular."

He drew a sheet of paper towards him and began to write out the order for release.[1]

> "The Warder in charge,
>
> "Lerwick Gaol.
>
> "In accordance with instructions I have received from the Admiralty I hereby authorise you to release all those members of the Post Office Staff including two mail gig drivers that you have in your custody; this order will take effect at once.
>
> "(Sgd.) H.C.Evans, Lieut. Colonel.

Evans then walked up to the prison and delivered the order personally.

---

[1]   Letter from J. Devon to Sir James Dodds, dated 7th November, 1914 quoting Evans' order for release – NAS, HH31/17

Warder Morrison was delighted to get the order. He took it immediately to the postmaster and then announced to all of the staff that they were free to go.

"If you will just collect your belongings and come downstairs I will complete the formalities and you can go," said Morrison. "It's all right William, you can come and collect your gramophone and records later when you get hold of a handcart."

The staff were astounded.

"Did you get any reason yet, why we were arrested and why they are now letting us go?" asked someone.

"No. No reason at all for anything," said the warder.

"What on earth has it all been about?" asked George Manson. "It makes absolutely no sense."

"Sense or nonsense, I'm off home," said a voice. "Before old Evans changes his mind again."

"Wait," said Mr Macmaster. "Before you all go I want to say two things. First I want to thank Warder Morrison for the way he has treated us all."

There was a murmur of agreement and thanks from the rest.

"Next, I want to make sure that none of you go back to the Post Office until I have spoken to the Surveyor and made sure that we will get a full apology from the military authorities."

The staff were in agreement over this, too.

"I will let you know what has been decided," said the postmaster.

It was 10.55 in the morning when Warder Morrison released the thirty-two remaining members of staff. In a very short time the men were making their way home. As they came out of the prison they saw surprise and relief cross the faces of those in the street.

"What's this?" shouted a voice. "A prison break-out?"

"We've just been released!"

The news spread like wildfire through the town.

Hug walked through the front door of number 12.

"You're early from the post office," said Leebie.

"I haven't been to the post office today," said Hug. "We've all been released."

Leebie's knees gave way under her and she sat down in a chair with a bang.

"I can't believe it," she said and burst into tears.

Hug picked up Jessie and said, "But it's true. We are all out now." This has been hard on Leebie, he thought. She looked tired and ill. Jean and Johnny were dancing a jig in the middle of the floor.

"I'll better go and tell Mam," said Johnny and shot out of the front door leaving it open. They heard his shoes clattering on the stones outside.

"We still have not got any explanation for this," said Hug. "Not one word about anything," he said bitterly.

Warder Morrison composed a lengthy telegram to the Prison Commissioners in Edinburgh. He sent a copy of the order he had received from Evans and added:

"The Officer Commanding Troops delivered this order personally and the 32 Post Office officials were set at liberty at 10.55 a.m. this forenoon. All was done quietly and good order prevailed."

When the telegram was received in Edinburgh, the Prison Commission sent a telegram to the Secretary for Scotland informing him of what had happened.[2]

The telegram was sent at 1.32 pm and read:

"Lerwick post office prisoners all liberated this morning by order of officer commanding troops in accordance with instructions received him from Admiralty. Letter to follow. Prison Commission Edinburgh."

Mr. Jas. Devon wrote to the Under Secretary for Scotland, Sir James Dodds.

> "Dear Sir,
> In continuation of their letter of the 5th instant, the Prison Commissioners have the honour to subjoin, for the information of the Secretary for Scotland, a copy of a telegram just received from the Warder in Charge of Lerwick Prison : -"

He enclosed a copy and sent the letter.

In London, another file was opened in the Secretary for Scotland's department. Headed 'Prison Commissioners', the subject was stated as 'Arrest of Post Office

---

2   Telegram dated 7th November, 1914 – NAS – HH31/17.

The telegraph announcing the liberation of the prisoners.

National Archives of Scotland

> **POST OFFICE TELEGRAPHS.**
>
> N.B.—This Form must accompany any inquiry respecting this Telegram.
>
> If the Receiver of an Inland Telegram doubts its accuracy, he may have it repeated on payment of half the amount originally paid for its transmission, any fraction of 1d. less than ½d. being reckoned as ½d.; and if it be found that there was any inaccuracy, the amount paid for repetition will be refunded. Special conditions are applicable to the repetition of Foreign Telegrams.
>
> Office of Origin and Service Instructions.
>
> Charges to pay
>
> Office Stamp
>
> Handed in at — Received here at
>
> Edinburgh
>
> TO { Albyn Earl Lan
>
> Lerwick post office prisoners all liberated this morning by order of officer commanding troops in accordance with instructions received him from Admiralty letter prison Commission Edinburgh

Officials at Lerwick.' It was handed first to a senior member of staff to study before being passed to the Under Secretary for Scotland.[3]

"This is a curious episode," he noted on the cover, "& one not likely to enhance the popularity of the "Services" in Shetland.

"I am not clear on what authority these people were confined in prison. I could understand their being taken into military custody but confinement in a civil prison is another matter. However, we do not know the facts yet & it is for the authority which acted & not for us to justify what has been done."

At the Admiralty a short note was being written to the Secretary for Scotland's department.[4]

7th Nov. 1914

Dear Mr Smith

We sent a telegram yesterday to the Vice-Admiral directing him to release the Postal Staff at Lerwick unless the investigation showed that any individual was guilty. In the latter case of course the individual could be retained in custody.

---

3   File cover, Secretary for Scotland, no. 25478/1283 – NAS, HH31/17.
4   Handwritten note dated 7th November, 1914 – NAS, HH31/17.

7 Nov. 1814

Dear Mr Smith

I sent a telegram yesterday to the Vice Admiral directing him to release the Postal Staff at Berwick unless the investigation showed that any individual was guilty. In the latter case I came the

individual would be retained in custody.

The enquiry so far as I can see does not throw very much light on the matter but there is evidently no reason for suspecting that any large number of the Staff have been guilty of tampering with

the letters — if indeed any have. But so far the enquiry has not thrown any conclusion — some of the opened covers being here — and until it is complete it is not possible to speak definitely. Anyhow I hope all the innocent people will spend their Sabbath

out of Gaol.

Yours truly

J. W. Evans

Letter from Evans to Mr Smith about the enquiry.　　　　　*National Archives of Scotland*

The enquiry so far as can be seen does not throw very much light on the matter but there is evidently no reason for suspecting that any large number of the staff have been guilty of tampering with the letters – if indeed any have. But so far the enquiry has not been very exhaustive – some of the opened covers being here – and until it is completed it is not possible to speak definitely. Anyhow I hope all the innocent people will spend their Sabbath out of Gaol.

Yours truly
J.M. Evans.

People passing by the jail in Lerwick that evening heard no music or laughter. There were fewer lights shining. Gloom was settling over the building once more. It was business as usual.

The laughter and merriment had shifted to the homes of the ex-prisoners. Celebrations were the order of the day. Hug was thankful to be home to look after the family again and especially Leebie. She would not recover from the shock for a long time. Her hair would remain white.

The postmaster's mood, however, was far from content. He had had a visit from the Post Office Surveyor, Mr Dunlop, and his colleague.[5]

"Dunlop had the effrontery to assume that we would all just go back to work tomorrow as if nothing had happened," he said to his wife.

"That is not very sympathetic, to say the least," said Mrs Macmaster.

"I told him that there would be no return until we had a full explanation and an apology."

"Do you think you will get that?"

"We had better. This has been an insult to us all."

---

5   Letter from Macmaster to Manson, dated 24th January 1957.

CHAPTER 15

Sunday, 8th November, 1914

THE POST OFFICE STAFF, thankful to be released from prison, spent Sunday quietly at home, glad to be with their families again. The staff were happy to be free once more, although the experience of being in jail had not been so very dreadful. There had been comfort in numbers and indeed at times a kind of holiday spirit had prevailed. The fact that they did not know why they had been arrested and the uncertainty of what was to happen to them had been the hardest things to bear. The cramped conditions were negligible compared to that.

In many ways it had been a much greater strain on all of the families involved. They had had to supply all the food, walking to and from the prison in harsh weather. They had had no idea of the reason for the arrests. They had had to listen to rumours and speculation about the guilt or otherwise of the men and the fact that they were accused of spying. They had lived with the knowledge that the men could be executed. Their situation was much worse.

These first few months of the war had been full of alarms of espionage. It seemed every day's newspaper contained stories of spies. Forty spies, for example, were reported to have been caught and shot in Belgium. The Post Office staff in the prison may have had faith in the fact that they were innocent and would therefore be released sooner or later. Their families, even though they knew the men were innocent, did not have the same faith in their eventual release. The families were terrified that the men would be shot.

And so it was that the released men could be happy again almost straight away but their families would take much longer to recover.

Mr Macmaster called a meeting of senior Post Office staff.[1] They met at his home in the afternoon to discuss the question of when to return to work. The Postmaster explained that Mr Dunlop had approached him and requested that the staff return to work immediately. He did not feel that they should, until they had been given a public apology by the military authority for their arrest. The men agreed with him, wholeheartedly, about the need for an apology but felt that the longer they stayed away from work, the bigger the muddle in the Post Office would become.

"It's your decision," said Macmaster. "I will go along with whatever you feel is best."

The decision was made to return to work the next day.

Later Mr Macmaster confided to his wife that he was disappointed.

"I was hoping that they would not return until an apology was forthcoming," he said to his wife. "However, they are all very loyal to the Post Office – dedicated to it really. Which is good. We can still insist that we get an apology and maybe some compensation for the treatment they and their families had to endure.

"You know," he added, "I can't believe that it is just a week ago today that we were all arrested. It seems more like a lifetime."

"You took a dreadful risk," said Mrs Macmaster. "What if one of the men had been found guilty? At best you would have lost your job and at worst … Oh! It doesn't bear thinking about."

"You know I could not have left my staff to face that alone. And in any case I had absolute faith in them."

"Faith in them might not have been enough. The way this whole affair has been conducted I am astonished that they did not find someone guilty just to prove that they had done the right thing."

"No, no," said Mr Macmaster. "They would never do that in this country."

"Are you sure?" asked Mrs Macmaster. "Are you really sure?"

The Under Secretary for Scotland was studying the report compiled by the Scottish Office about the arrest of the Lerwick Post Office staff. He read the comment written by the senior official and noted underneath;[2]

"Yes. I heard about this in Edinburgh and saw the Secretary to the Post Office, the Prison Commissioners, Mr Crombie, and discussed the legality of it with the two law officers. Anyhow the men are out now," he added dismissively.

---

1   Letter from Macmaster to Manson, dated 24th January 1957.
2   File cover, Secretary for Scotland, no. 25478/1283 – NAS, HH31/17.

Mr Crombie sat in his hotel room, collating his notes and beginning to write his report for the Prison Commissioners

CHAPTER 16

Monday, 9th November, 1914

ON MONDAY MORNING the Lerwick Post Office staff returned to work and the relief staff from Aberdeen prepared for the journey south.

The staff found that there was still a backlog of work. Although the Aberdeen staff had managed to deal with a lot of it there was still confusion in some departments, the sorting office being most in need of attention. There were quite a lot of empty mailbags, which had all to be turned inside out. Out of one of them, which had been returned from the naval base at Swarbacks Minn, fell a small sealed canvas bag addressed to the Commanding Officer.

"Here, what's this?" said the sorter. "This has never been opened. It's still sealed."

"Is it indeed?" said the man next to him. "Who is it addressed to?"

"The Commanding Officer at Swarbacks Minn. You don't suppose this it what they were looking for?"

"It might well be," said the other grimly. "They've returned the bag with that in it."

"I'll better take it to the Postmaster."

Mr Macmaster examined the sealed package.

"I think I had better take this to the Post Office officials from headquarters. They are still here."

Mr Crombie was writing up his report from the notes he had made the previous day. In his official report he recorded the events of Sunday, 1st November, beginning with the arrival of Lt Col Evans at the prison at 1.30 pm. He wrote that Evans had told Warder Morrison to expect 25 prisoners and had given him no details of who they were.

Crombie's account was meticulous.[1] Every action that Warder Morrison had taken was recorded and he noted particularly that the warder had asked the men what they were charged with and that none of them knew. He took great pains to show that Warder Morrison had acted correctly at all times and that the prisoners had been treated according to Evans' instructions, which were that they were to be considered, not as prisoners, but as under arrest. He wrote down the exact numbers of men in each cell and the size of the cells.

The last part of his report included details of how the men had spent their time and the privileges that they had been allowed. He noted that the postmaster had refused to use anything but prison bedding although the others had their own bedding from home. He mentioned the fact that the men could write and receive as many letters as they liked, but that all of them were read on the instructions of Evans.

He finished with a note that they were allowed two exercise periods when the weather, which was very bad, had permitted and that it was at their discretion to decide when they returned inside.

With this report he included a copy of Evans' order committing the men to prison and a further copy of the warder's 'Daily Statement of Post Office Officials under Detention, and Prisoners Male and Female in custody at this Prison'.[2]

When he had finished this report to his satisfaction, Mr Crombie, mindful of his unofficial instructions, began a second, confidential report. This contained information of a very different kind.

It started with the arrival of HMS *Sappho* bearing the instructions from Vice-Admiral Sir Stanley Colville to arrest the Lerwick Post Office staff. He described how Cdr Startin had arrived at the church with the orders and the subsequent actions of Evans in rounding up the staff and marching them to prison.[3]

He continued:

"To the Postmaster alone he stated that secret correspondence for the Fleet passing through Lerwick P.O. had been tampered with and that he had received confidential instructions to arrest the staff and detain them pending investigation."

He recorded the fact that most of the Post Office officials' houses were searched by Col Evans' men.

---

1   Official report by D. Crombie – NAS, HH31/17.
2   Copy of Warder's daily report – NAS, HH31/17.
3   Confidential report by D. Crombie – NAS, HH31/17.

"Food had to be taken three times a day to the prison by the friends," he wrote, "which caused much indignation and comment amongst the people.

"The last of the men were discharged on Saturday 7th at 11 am by order of Col Evans without the men ever having been informed on what grounds they were imprisoned or why they were discharged out of custody.

"I understand that they were discharged on a telegram stating that expert opinion did not support the view that the Admiralty correspondence had been tampered with.

"Mr Macmaster, on behalf of himself and his Staff, called on me to express their high appreciation of the treatment received in prison, and their thanks to Warder Morrison for making their lot as tolerable as he could under the circumstances. The overcrowding of which he complained he knew was unavoidable and beyond Warder Morrison's power to remedy with the number of cells at his disposal.

"Colonel Evans, whom I saw, says that in arresting the staff, he was acting on confidential instructions from the Vice-Admiral of the Orkneys and Shetland, and that he sent them to Lerwick Prison as being the only suitable place in Lerwick for their proper and safe detention. I informed him we are desirous of assisting as much as we can other Government Departments, but it seemed to me that they might have been detained in the Fort, the Territorial Drill Hall, the Town Hall, a Church or some other Hall, and spared the indignity of being sent to a common prison. He replied that he did not consider the sanitary and other arrangements at these places were adequate and the Fort was inconvenient. I then ventured to say that the procedure did not seen to be quite in terms of Reg. No. 13 – 2 para., but he naturally declined to express any view on that point.

"I think Warder Morrison's action in the emergency was satisfactory, but, considering the number to be received, he should, perhaps, before admitting the men, have wired the Commissioners for instructions. It must be noted, however, that Warder Morrison could obtain no information from Col Evans as to the exact number to be received, who the prisoners were or what they were charged with. The legality of detaining them in prison will no doubt be considered by the Commissioners.

"So far as our Department is concerned I feel satisfied as much as possible was done for the comfort and convenience of the men.

"The arrest and marching of the men through the streets and the parade thrice daily of respectable people taking food to the prison have aroused a feeling of intense indignation among the people. Some of the leading citizens, including the Provost, called on the Sheriff, asking if something could not be done, but of course he declined to advise. The people regard the incident as an insult to their quiet little town, and a serious aspersion on their good name and character.

"D. Crombie,

"Inspector

"9th November, 1914."

Underneath he added a postscript to the effect that he had shown the Post Office Surveyor, Mr Dunlop, over the prison as had been arranged with the Undersecretary for Scotland and let him take measurements of the cells.

When Mr Macmaster showed the package which had been found in the empty mailbag to the Post Office officials from Headquarters they decided that it should be returned to the naval base at Swarbacks Minn.[4]

"I think we should return this immediately," said Mr Dunlop. "Come with us, Postmaster, and we will see if this is what they were looking for."

When they reached Swarbacks Minn they were taken on board the flagship to see the Commanding Officer. They handed over the bag to him.

"This was found inside an empty mailbag which had been returned from here," said Mr Dunlop. "We thought it should be brought to you straight away in view of the events of the last week."

The CO opened the bag and looked at the contents.

"These are not important," he said, "but thank you for bringing them back. I do apologise for the trouble caused by the carelessness of my officers. They should have inspected the mailbag more carefully. I will of course reprimand them over this."

The Postmaster and the two from headquarters returned to Lerwick none the wiser. If that package, returned unopened from Swarbacks Minn, was not the missing letter, then what was? Why the arrest? And equally why were they released? Was the Commanding Officer pretending the letter was unimportant to cover up the fact that it was they, themselves, to blame for the fact that it had gone missing? The mystery grew, if anything, deeper.

---

4   Memo in a letter from Macmaster to Manson, dated 24th January 1957, regarding Swarbacks
    Minn incident on 9th November, 1914

Mr Macmaster returned from this unsatisfactory trip to the base more determined than ever to get an explanation and an apology from the naval authorities.

"And it must be a public apology," he vowed.

CHAPTER 17

November, December, 1914

ON 11TH NOVEMBER Sheriff McLennan wrote from Edinburgh to Sir James Dodds at the Scottish Office in London informing him that the prisoners had been released from the jail in Lerwick.[1] He added that he had still no information on the reason for the arrest. The Shetland papers, he said, had maintained absolute silence on the affair. There had been no mention of it in the latest paper he had received from Lerwick.

Sir James Dodds replied the next day from Whitehall.

"Yes, we know about the Lerwick affair," he said, "and its somewhat lame and impotent conclusion. Thanks for your note."

On the 14th November the Prison Commission in Edinburgh sent a copy of Mr. Crombie's confidential report to the Scottish Office in London.[2] A memo, entitled 'Committal to Prison of the Lerwick Post Office staff', was circulated rapidly among senior officials. On the cover a comment had been added to the effect that the Prison Commissioners were of the opinion that these persons should have been detained under military guard, but having been sent to prison they considered it their duty to do their best to accommodate them. Underneath Sir James Dodds had initialled his added comment.[3]

"I think we should communicate the Prison Commissioners' view to the Admiralty."

On Monday, 16th November, at Question Time, Mr George Terrell, MP, rose to ask the Postmaster General, Mr Hobhouse, whether any, and if any, how many of the

---

1   Letter from Sheriff McLennan dated 11th November, 1914 – NAS, HH31/17.
2   Dodds reply – NAS, HH31/17.
3   File cover – Secretary for Scotland, no. 25478/1376 – NAS, HH31/17.

employees in the Scottish postal and telegraph service were of German or Austrian nationality in origin, and the dates of their respective appointments.[4]

The Postmaster General replied that there were no persons of German or Austrian nationality employed in the Scottish postal and telegraph service, but there were thirty-one British subjects so employed whose parents or one or other of them were German or Austrian. The dates of their respective appointments were, for the most part, not recorded in London, and could only be furnished after inquiry in Scotland.

Mr Hobhouse stated further that censorship was the responsibility of the military and not the Post Office.

Mr Macmaster was far from satisfied with the response to his demand for an apology. No apology had been received and to add insult to injury he discovered that Post Office headquarters were refusing to pay the staff their wages for the week they had been in prison. They had not been working so therefore they were not entitled to be paid.

"This is the outside of enough," he said and began a series of furious communications by telegraph and letter. After a considerable length of time he succeeded in his quest. The Post Office finally acknowledged that the staff had been unable to work through no fault of their own and therefore they were to be paid.

"That's something at least," he said. "Now we start the battle for a public apology."

Later that day he had occasion to speak to Hug Tait and asked him if he thought the staff were satisfied with their treatment, arrest and subsequent release without any reasons given for either.

"Not in the least," said Hug. "It is a little better now that you have managed to get their pay for them, but they are still very angry about it all."

"Do you remember, about this time last year, we were reading in *The Scotsman* about that incident in – where was it?"

"In Zabern," said Hug. "The military there were very high-handed in the way they dealt with the population. Definitely exceeded their authority."

"I said that couldn't happen in Britain, didn't I?" said Macmaster ruefully.

The remainder of the momentous year, 1914, saw the beginning of the campaign to clear their names.

---

4   *Hansard*, vol.68 – 16th November 1914, p. 219.

CHAPTER 18

January, 1915

JANUARY saw the beginning of a series of discussions between government departments as to whether compensation should be paid to the Lerwick Post office staff, and if so, how much. Mr Macmaster had presented his views and the views of his staff on their arrest and imprisonment forcefully to Post Office headquarters. Nothing short of a public and published apology would satisfy them, but they made no claim for compensation. They wanted an explanation and to be told the reason for their arrest and subsequent release. Money would be no substitute for having their names cleared, for being shown to be innocent before the world.

The Admiralty, however, continued to think that throwing money at the problem would help to make it go away.

On 8th January Mr Masterton Smith wrote from the Admiralty to the Prime Minister's private secretary, Mr Bonham Carter, enclosing a memorandum regarding an incident that, in his words, had "caused a considerable stir in the Post Office world."[1] He was recommending that a small sum be paid in compensation to the staff concerned and requested that Bonham Carter put the case to the Prime Minister and ask that he sanction payment from the Prime Minister's Fund as suggested by the Treasury.

The memorandum read as follows:

"In October last the Commander-in-Chief, Home Fleets, telegraphed that a registered letter addressed to him containing important secret matter had been opened in the post, the two outer envelopes having been opened by steaming and the third inside sealed envelope cut open leaving the seal

---

1   Letter plus memo – National Archives (Kew), T1/11742.

intact. As this was not the only case, and suspicion pointed very strongly to the Lerwick Post Office as responsible, drastic measures were considered necessary. Orders were according issued for the arrest of the whole of the staff, which was duly carried out.

"Investigation, however, proved their innocence of the charge, but not before all members of the staff had passed some time in Lerwick gaol. A letter of regret has been sent but it is thought that some pecuniary compensation should be made in recognition of the discomfort and indignity which they have had to endure. A gratuity to the extent of two days' pay for each day spent in gaol is considered to be an adequate solatium.

"The standing Emergency Committee at the Treasury have expressed the view that such a grant is not properly chargeable to Naval Funds, and have suggested that it should be borne by the Prime Minister's Fund or by the Civil Contingencies Fund.

"The amount required to provide compensation on the basis set forth to the employees will be £104. 11. 0.

"It may be added, as showing that there was strong prima facie evidence justifying the drastic action taken, that though the Post Office officials have satisfied the Admiralty that the letters were not tampered with, the Commander-in-Chief, Home Fleets, has not yet been convinced."

This memorandum created a flurry of activity in various departments of Government. A note from the Treasury, written by Lord Cross to the Admiralty, asked for information on the amount to be paid, noting that the Naval Emergency Committee had said it was not an appropriate charge for the Admiralty Vote.[2] It added that: "The Post Office say that the P.M.G. interviewed Wason M.P. and (they believe) promised compensation. If anything is to be given it will presumably have to come out of Special Services Fund. Will you advise as to how much, if anything."

A further note instructed Lord Cross to find out the Post Office view from one of their Private Secretaries.

On 19th January Lord Cross wrote to the Post Office asking if, in their view, "these men should receive compensation for having been locked up, and if so what is the amount which the Post Office think should be awarded to each? Is it considered that the compensation if any is to be a charge on the Post Office Vote?"[3]

---

2   Handwritten note – National Archives, T1/11742.
3   Letter to P. Shears – National Archives, T1/11742.

On 20th January Mr Gardiner from the Post Office replied in unequivocal terms.

"1. The grant of compensation was settled by the Cabinet and the Postmaster General has announced to the public that it will be paid.
"2. The Admiralty proposal, namely two days' pay for each day's imprisonment, seems to be fair.
"3. The decision of the Cabinet was that compensation should be paid out of Naval funds."

On 28th January a note from the Treasury to Mr Davies, private secretary to the First Lord of the Admiralty stated bluntly that the Postmaster General was prepared to agree to the expenditure being defrayed from any source other than the Post Office Vote. It was thought that the Cabinet did not consider alternative methods of charge. Therefore the suggestion of using the Special Services Fund should be acted upon and the only question remaining to be answered was whether the Treasury considered the scale of the compensation proposed was fair.

Underneath was written a terse addition.

"Quite so. There is no Treasury reason for objecting to the amount."

Finally Mr Bonham Carter wrote a memorandum to the Prime Minister recommending payment, putting forward the Treasury's view that the sum of money involved was not properly chargeable to the Navy Vote and should therefore be paid from the Civil Contingencies Fund or the Special Services Fund.[4]

He added, however, a further thought on the subject.

"The Civil Contingencies Fund seems to have supplied such grants, at any rate in the recent past, but it is improbable that the case will recur at all often and the application need hardly be refused on the ground of precedent. The accounts for the Civil Contingencies Fund are presented to Parliament, and if the gratuity is paid from that Fund the matter is more likely to be raised in the House than if the Special Services Fund is used. If you think that this is undesirable, there seems no objection to making a grant from the Special Services Fund."

A hand-written note at the top of the memorandum, dated 9/2/15 stated, "Agree to sum being paid from S.S.F."

---

4   Memo to PM – National Archives, T1/11742.

CHAPTER 19

February, 1915

THROUGHOUT FEBRUARY correspondence between governmental departments on the subject of the compensation to be paid to the Lerwick Post Office staff continued to flow. From the moment that the Admiralty admitted that it had made a mistake in arresting the staff there seemed to be general agreement that compensation should be paid. How it should be paid and by which department was the main point of discussion.

The General Post Office considered that the staff should definitely be given some monetary award for the hardships they had endured, but was adamant that the money should not be paid by them. The Prime Minister and the Cabinet were equally anxious that the award should be paid out of some fund which did not necessitate a debate in the House of Commons. The Admiralty were refusing to pay it out of the Admiralty Vote.

Eventually it was agreed that it should be paid out of the Special Services Fund and this was ratified on 15th February.[1]

On 19th February a letter was sent from the Admiralty to the General Post Office to inform the Postmaster General of the steps being taken to make reparation to the staff for their wrongful arrest.[2]

> Admiralty
> 19th. February, 1915.
>
> Sir,
>
> With reference to previous correspondence relative to the alleged tampering with correspondence between the Admiralty and the

---

[1] Civil List Grants – file no. 4321 – National Archives, T1/11742.
[2] Copy of Admiralty letter dated 19th February, 1915 – The British Postal Museum & Archive.

Commander-in-Chief, Home Fleets, I am commanded by My Lords Commissioners of the Admiralty to acquaint you, for the information of His Majesty's Postmaster General, that they are satisfied that the condition in which the particular letters were received, was not due to any improper proceedings on the part of any member of the Postal Staff at Lerwick and that the complete innocence of the whole staff has been proved.

2. I am commanded therefore by Their Lordships to request that you will inform the Postmaster and Postal Staff at Lerwick that the subsequent investigation of the charge brought against them has proved their complete innocence in the matter, and that you will express Their Lordships' regret that unfounded suspicion should have been cast upon them.

3. I am to add that as compensation for the indignity and discomfort endured by the Lerwick Postal Staff in November last, Their Lordships desire, if the Postmaster General sees no objection, to make a grant of two days' pay to each member of the staff in respect of each day spent under arrest.

I am, Sir,

Your obedient Servant,

(signed) O. MURRAY.

On 23rd February Cathcart Wason finally managed to put a question to the Postmaster General at a sitting in Parliament.[3] He asked the Postmaster General "if he is now in a position to state what measures he is prepared to take with reference to the outrage on his officers at Lerwick last November, when they were arrested and marched through the town to the common gaol, where there was no reasonable accommodation for the number"?

Mr Hobhouse replied: "I am glad to be able to say that the Admiralty have now informed me that the investigation which they have conducted into the charges against the Postmaster and the Post Office staff at Lerwick has proved the complete innocence of all officials. The Admiralty express their regret that unfounded suspicion should have been cast upon them, and propose to make a pecuniary grant as compensation."

A few days later, on the 26th, a memo written from the GPO to the Postmaster General cast further light on the subject and seemed to suggest that it had reached a satisfactory conclusion and that the matter was now closed.[4]

3   *Hansard*, vol. 70, p.174.
4   26th February 1915 – memo – The British Postal Museum & Archive.

An extract from
Hansard *in February
1915 with a question
from Shetland MP
Cathcart Wason about
the Post Office
'outrage'.*

Lerwick Post Office (Innocence of Staff Proved).

20. **Mr. CATHCART WASON** asked the Postmaster-General if he is now in a position to state what measures he is prepared to take with reference to the outrage on his officers at Lerwick last November, when they were arrested and marched through the town to the common gaol, where there was no reasonable accommodation for the number?

The **POSTMASTER-GENERAL** (Mr. Hobhouse): I am glad to be able to say that the Admiralty have now informed me that the investigation which they have conducted into the charges against the Postmaster and the Post Office staff at Lerwick has proved the complete innocence of all officials. The Admiralty express their regret that unfounded suspicion should have been cast upon them, and propose to make a pecuniary grant as compensation.

"The Postmaster General,

I submit the papers dealing with the arrest of the Post Office staff at the instance of the Admiralty on the suspicion of tampering with secret correspondence for the Fleet.

The arrest was carried out on the afternoon of Sunday the 1st November, 40 members of the local staff being marched to the county jail with an escort of blue-jackets with fixed bayonets. They were confined in the cells with insufficient air space until, as the results of urgent representations to the Prison Commissioners in Edinburgh, 7 were released on the 4th November reducing the number in each cell to the proper complement.

It was ascertained that the suspicion of the Admiralty rested on the case of one letter alone. The cover of this letter was inspected in London by officers of the Investigation Branch of the Post Office who formed the opinion that the letter had not been tampered with at all. This view was accepted by the War Office and the Admiralty and instructions were issued by telegraph that the staff should be released unless local enquiry showed any individual to be guilty.

Accordingly, the whole staff were released at 11 am on Saturday the 7th. November.

The staff who behaved in a most exemplary manner under very trying circumstances were naturally anxious that some reparation should be made for the indignity suffered by them; and strong representations were made by Captain Norton to Dr. Macnamara with a view to an apology being offered and compensation being awarded. After considerable delay the Admiralty now announce that they are prepared to make a grant of two days' pay to each member of the staff in respect of each day spent under arrest; and they have written the enclosed letter expressing regret for the unfounded suspicion cast upon the staff.

I think that these steps will adequately meet the case; and I propose to have a notice in the terms of the attached draft exhibited publicly in the Lerwick Office.

Special credit is due to the Postmaster, Mr. Macmaster, for the way in which he handled the staff, especially in view of the fact that an attempt was made by the local coastguard officials who effected the arrest to induce him to accept more favourable treatment than the rest of the staff; and I propose to commend him especially in your name for his conduct throughout the incident.

R.M.
26 February, 1915.

Detention of the staff of the Lerwick Post Office
at the instance of the Admiralty.

The Lords Commissioners of the Admiralty have informed the Postmaster General that the complete innocence of all the members of the Lerwick Post Office staff has been proved and they have expressed their regret that unfounded suspicion should have been cast upon them. The Lords Commissioners have decided to make a pecuniary grant as compensation to each officer concerned.

The Postmaster General desires to record his satisfaction that the innocence of the staff has been established and his appreciation of their conduct in trying circumstances."

CHAPTER 20

Aftermath, 1915, March to August

MR MACMASTER was on holiday in the south of England, in Bournemouth, when the Postmaster General replied to Cathcart Wason's question in the House of Commons.[1] He was far from being satisfied with his answer and indeed the attitude it displayed towards the whole affair; it seemed to him that the Postmaster General considered that offering the staff a sum of money would be enough to settle the matter. To Mr Macmaster that was adding insult to injury. He telegraphed Hug Tait at the Lerwick Post Office to tell him that he was far from satisfied at the outcome. He did not want to influence the staff's decision on whether to accept the Admiralty's offer. He felt that that was up to each man to decide.

On 5th March Mr Herbert Wooster, Surveyor at the General Post Office, sent a letter to each member of the imprisoned staff with a copy of the letter from the Lords Commissioners of the Admiralty to the Postmaster General.[2] The staff at Lerwick felt that this was a step in the right direction. The Admiralty had admitted that they were innocent of the charges against them but they had still not been informed precisely the nature of those charges. The Admiralty had apologised certainly, but offering the staff a sum of money for the indignity of being falsely imprisoned was a bit like fobbing the natives off with a string of beads.

"I am certainly not accepting their offer," said Hug after telling Leebie of this latest development. "How on earth can they imagine that offering us money will compensate in any fashion for what they have done!"

1   Letter from Macmaster to George Manson dated 4th April, 1958.
2   Copy of letter dated 5th March, 1915 – The British Postal Museum & Archive.

"Are you refusing it for all of the staff?" asked Leebie.

"No. I can't do that. They will all have to make up their minds for themselves. It's up to them. I can't tell them what to do. But I do know that most of them seem pretty disgusted at the idea that they can be bought off, as it were."

"Well, I can think of one or two who might take the money, you know," said Leebie. "Their wives will maybe talk them into it. The money would be a godsend to them."

"That's up to them," said Hug. "No-one would blame them at all. In fact I don't suppose anyone would know in any case. Everybody has to apply individually to the Post Office. And we won't be asking one another if we have applied either."

When Mr Macmaster returned from holiday he immediately began to protest through Post Office channels about the apology and compensation offered by the Admiralty. He considered both to be completely inadequate and a further cause for grievance was the fact that the staff, including himself, now had criminal records after spending a week in jail. He wanted those records expunged as soon as possible. Thus began a long and bitter campaign, which was to result in the transfer of Mr Macmaster from Lerwick and a permanent record of the names of all the staff imprisoned.

In April a memo was sent from the GPO to the Postmaster General as follows:[3]

"The Post Office staff at Lerwick are not satisfied with the apology and compensation tendered to them on behalf of the Admiralty in connexion with their arrest in November last. Their views are voiced by the Postmaster who asks that the circumstances which led to the arrest may be fully stated to them, that compensation be awarded on the scale usual in the case of the wrongful arrest of civilians, that any prison records of their incarceration be expunged and that the facts be made public in the Post Office Circular.

"Mr. J. Cathcart Wason, M.P., who has been approached in the matter by the National Joint Committee of Postal and Telegraph Associations, has also written to ask whether it is true as alleged that in the case of certain members of the Staff the compensation offered is less than the amount which they could, and probably would, have earned in extra duty if they had not been arrested.

"It may be said at once that the latter allegation is not correct. The compensation offered is in every case in excess, generally considerably in

---

3   Memo to Postmaster General – The British Postal Museum & Archive.

excess of any sum which could have been earned by extra work performed over and above the normal duty; and as regards the prison records Mr Kirkwood has already received a promise that these shall be expunged. It is of course impossible to comply with the request that the Staff be informed of the circumstances which led to the arrest; and I think it is undesirable that any reference should be made to the case in the Post Office Circular. Any such reference could scarcely fail to have the effect of lowering the prestige of the Admiralty in the eyes of the Staff while on the other hand it is difficult to see in what way it could benefit the individuals concerned. Adequate publicity has already been given to the vindication of their innocence in the Press and in the Service Journals.

"I submit that the Postmaster be informed of the cancellation of the prison records and told that while you greatly regret the annoyance and vexation occasioned to him and to his staff it is not practicable for you to take any further action in this matter.

"Mr Cathcart Wason might be answered as follows:-

Arrest of Lerwick staff.

I have had enquiry made on the point raised in your letter of the 7th instant and I find that there is no ground for the allegation that the compensation awarded by the Admiralty is in any case less than the amount which the men concerned could have earned by performing extra duty after official hours.

The letter addressed to you by the National Joint Committee is returned herewith.

Two notes were added to this draft in the margin. The first read "Add that the prison record is expunged."

The second note is more serious. It reads:

"I regret to learn that another case of supposed tampering with Naval correspondence has occurred at Lerwick. – Mr. P. Robertson, a Sorting Clerk and Telegraphist being under strong suspicion of divulging the contents of a telegram. I will submit a report as soon as possible; but as Mr. Robertson was not in the office at the time of the arrest in November, I am not delaying the submission of this minute."

Peter Robertson had been posted to Sandwick at the outbreak of war. When the staff were arrested he was one of those recalled to the Lerwick Post Office when

Jimmy Williamson was left in charge. After the staff had been released Jimmy Williamson went back to duty with the Territorial Force but Peter had been released to remain at Lerwick. He had friends still among the Territorials and he still took a great interest in what was happening to them. He heard that they were to be posted to France and was therefore surprised to read, in an incoming telegram, that they were not going after all. Later, when his friends were discussing going to the front, they teased Peter, saying "Don't you wish you were going with us?"

Peter could not hold his tongue. "You're not going," he said. "I know you're not going."

It seems strange that this episode should be called 'tampering with Naval correspondence', let alone being called 'another case'. However the contents of a telegram were confidential and should not have been disclosed.

The postmaster and staff at Lerwick persisted in their demands for an explanation of their arrest, for more adequate compensation, for the deletion of the prison records and for a public account of the incident to be published in the Post Office Circular. Mr Macmaster did not feel like giving up and keeping quiet about it all. The compensation was the least of it. Getting rid of the prison records was of paramount importance and none of them would become reconciled to events if no explanation was forthcoming.

In July a further memo was sent to the Postmaster General from the GPO. It submitted a further memorial from the postmaster and staff of the post office at Lerwick and went on to state:[4]

"The main points of their appeal are: -
"1. That they should be informed more precisely of the grounds on which their arrest was made.
"2. That a notice fully exonerating them from all suspicion of blame should be inserted in the Post Office Circular.
"3. That the compensation offered to each man should be a round sum and considerably larger than the amount (double pay for the period of imprisonment in addition to their Post Office pay) already offered by the Admiralty. Ten pounds to each man is suggested.
"4. The complete deletion of the entries in the prison records.

4   Memo July 1915 – The British Postal Museum & Archive.

"There has been considerable friction between the local naval and military officials and the Post Office Staff since the occurrence of November last but a member of the Surveying Staff recently visited Lerwick and was able to clear up most of the existing differences.

"The Postmaster (Mr. Macmaster) who not unnaturally felt a good deal incensed at the action taken against him was, it was thought, hardly likely to facilitate the restoration of amicable relations; and it has been arranged to transfer him to Wellingborough.[5] Under a new Chief the staff will be more likely to let matters rest; and I do not think it would be desirable to reopen the questions of compensation or publicity as desired by the memorialists.

"I submit that they be informed that you have considered their appeal; that having regard to the public interest it is impossible to give them fuller information on the circumstances which led up to their arrest, but that they may be assured that the sole reason for the arrest was the alleged tampering with mails referred to in the Admiralty letter of February 19th which established the innocence of the staff; that you regret that you would not feel justified in again approaching the Admiralty with a view to the offer of an increased amount of compensation; nor are you agreed to give further publicity to the matter by means of a notice in the Post Office Circular or otherwise.

"Mr. Kirkwood is making enquiries as to the exact nature of the deletion of the prison records and I propose to inform the memorialists that a further reply on this point will be sent to them in due course and that they may rest assured that the promise made will be adequately carried out."

Later in the same month James Devon of the Prison Commission for Scotland wrote to Sir James Dodds at the Scottish Office.[6] He reminded Sir James of the circumstances of the arrest of the Lerwick Post Office staff and said that although the rules were relaxed in their favour, nevertheless they had been prisoners and official records had, of necessity, been made. The staff, on release, had asked that the records be deleted and they had therefore been struck through with red ink. This however had not satisfied the staff who wanted the records removed in their entirety from the Prison Record Book.

---

5   Mr Macmaster refers in a letter to George Manson dated 24th January, 1957 to his transfer to Wellingborough saying that he was invited to go. He does not seem to be aware that he was being transferred deliberately.

6   Letter from Devon to Dodds – NAS, HH31/17.

He continued:

"It seems to me that these men are making a quite unnecessary fuss. I suppose they were innocent, and in that case they are in the same position as many men and women who are sent to prison pending proceedings, and who are subsequently liberated without trial or after being acquitted of the charge against them. In every case the fact is noted, not only of their admission, but of the reason for their discharge. It was matter of notoriety that these Postal officials had been arrested, and destroying any record of the fact will not alter the fact. None but duly authorised persons have access to our books, and it would be rather a strong measure to mutilate or destroy them in order to please anybody. At the same time I recognise that to all rules there are exceptions, and it may be that you will wish us to destroy the entries in question or as many of them as possible and, if so, of course, this will be done.

"I may be permitted to remark that if this matter had concerned the Post Office records, the person who proposed to alter them would be treated with a more summary refusal than we have given, but in these days above all days one wants to be the cause of as little strife as possible."

A handwritten note underneath records;

"I think you have acted properly and reasonably and quite agree with your last observation. 'Facts are chiels etc.' Surely the P.O. should be satisfied to know that when a record has been made a countermand of absolution has also been made."

It seemed as though none of the demands of the Post Office staff were to be met. To say that the staff were not satisfied by this would be a gross understatement. The struggle to clear their names continued.

The Postmaster General had studied the requests made by the Lerwick Post Office staff and noted in a memo that while there was every desire to meet their demands the circumstances did not allow this.[7] He concluded the memo by saying:

"I do not consider it would be advisable through a notice in the Post Office Circular or otherwise, to direct public attention again to the occurrence. I

---

7   The British Postal Museum & Archive.

can well understand the feelings of indignation and resentment which the treatment to which they were subjected must have aroused in the minds of the Lerwick staff, but their honour having been completely vindicated I trust that they will no longer dwell upon the injustice which they have suffered."

On 3rd August this sentiment is echoed in a letter to Sir James Dodds from G. Murray at the General Post Office.[8]

"The staff have been," he writes, "and are still, very much disturbed at their treatment, and the Postmaster General is anxious that everything possible should be done to soothe their feelings and prevent any public manifestation which they are now threatening. I understand the question of the prison records has been referred to the Secretary for Scotland, and I should be very much obliged if you would do what you can to ensure that the offending entries are entirely deleted."

On 5th August Mr Devon from the Prison Commission for Scotland sent a letter to Sir James explaining in great detail how the prison records were kept and the relevant entries made when prisoners were released.[9]

"There are many cases in the year," he noted, "of persons who are arrested on one charge or another and never brought to trial. The Register contains their names and particulars with the entry – 'Liberated by …' then follows the name of the authority. I daresay all of them have a grievance equal to that of the Post Office officials, but these gentlemen seem to have forgotten that in the process of moving for the deletion of their names, the whole business is kept alive, and documents with reference to it are multiplied. Even if the names are deleted, the mutilation of the books would require to be explained by some record giving the authority for their condition. The books are not open to the public and I don't believe the public are in the slightest degree interested in the question and would never suspect that these people were martyrs if they held their tongues about it."

Mr Devon mentioned also that he had requested copies of the prison records showing the arrest and detention of the Post Office staff in order to see how they could be amended.

---

8   NAS, HH31/17.
9   NAS, HH31/17.

CHAPTER 21

1915, August to September

MR MACMASTER left Lerwick in the beginning of August. He had not applied for promotion and was surprised to be offered the post at Wellingborough. It could not be said to be promotion although the salary was slightly more. It was a transfer, in effect.

"I am sorry to be leaving Lerwick," he said. "I have enjoyed being here in spite of spending some of the time in jail. And I am sorry to be going before the problem of compensation and an apology has been resolved. It is taking a long time and I feel that that is unjustified."

Before Mr Macmaster left the staff organised an evening's entertainment and as many staff as possible attended to show their appreciation for everything that the Postmaster had done for them. Messrs. Malcolmson & Co. provided the refreshments and after these had been served there were speeches.

The Shetland News reported Hug Tait's remarks.[1] He began by saying that the staff were sorry to lose Mr Macmaster and by praising the work he had done at Lerwick.

The report continued:

> "Mr. Macmaster has never at any time spared himself at the expense of his staff; in point of fact the reverse has been the case, and the kindness and generosity which he at all times extended to us has endeared him to the staff and has placed him very highly in their estimation; and I can assure Mr. Macmaster that no staff with which he has been connected will follow his future career with more interest or be happier to hear of his future advancement than the Lerwick staff. (Loud applause) One will always

---

1   *The Shetland News* 7th August, 1915.

remember that at the time of our memorable arrest he preferred to share a prison cell to be with his staff than lunch and be the guest of an Admiral. (Applause)"

Mrs Macmaster was not forgotten.

"One will not readily forget her sympathy with various officers' families during our incarceration, and the hopeful feeling left after her visit at a time when she must have felt her position most trying."

The report concluded:

"Mr. and Mrs. Macmaster left Lerwick by steamer on Monday evening amid thundering cheers from the balcony of the Post Office."

On 13th August Mr Devon wrote to Sir James on the subject of removing the Post Office officials' names from the prison register.[2]
He enclosed the papers showing the entries that had been made and added:

"I am also sending you a copy of the *Shetland News*, dated 7th instant, containing an account of a presentation to the Postmaster. From the proceedings, as reported, it would appear that the officials speak with two voices, glorifying their imprisonment with one and complaining of the indignity of having their names in the books with the other. They seem to wish the past to be forgotten and yet to be remembered with pride."

The correspondence between the Scottish Office and the Prison Commission rumbled on throughout August. The Scottish Office seemed to be of the opinion that it would be a good idea to remove the names of the Lerwick Post Office staff from the register, bodily if necessary by cutting out the pages if that were possible. The Prison Commission responded by enumerating the various volumes that these names had been mentioned in, such as the Criminal Register, the Gate Book, and the Governor's Journal among others.

2   Letter from Devon to Dodds – 13th August 1915 – NAS, HH31/17.

Suggestions were made as to the methods that might be employed to obliterate the names; taking out the pages or pasting them together.

On 20th August Sir James wrote to Mr Murray, secretary to the Postmaster General, telling him of the Prison Commission's decision to refuse to remove the names from the register.[3] They were sympathetic to the Postmaster General's desire that "everything possible should be done to soothe the feelings of these officers" but they considered that the records were inviolable. The men were in the same position as others arrested and subsequently released without being put on trial. In addition, if the names were obliterated or the pages removed an official explanation would have to be given for the mutilation of the book. Further, the facts were already in the public domain since they had been published in the press and had no doubt been recorded in the Post Office records.

"From the point of view of the officials themselves," he added, "the entries in the prison books are of value as constituting the official record of the fact that the discharge took place at the request of the naval authorities."

After this example of specious reasoning he concluded that altering prison records in Scotland would probably necessitate consulting the Lord Advocate on the legal aspect of the case.

This letter did not end the matter as he had hoped. Mr Murray replied in September from the General Post Office in quite sharp terms.[4] Whilst he agreed with Sir James on the difficulty of removing the names from the register, he hoped that it would be possible to record that the men were released "at the instance of the Admiralty, who expressed themselves satisfied that the charges against them were wholly unfounded.

"I think," he continued, "that the case of the Lerwick Staff does differ materially from that of other persons who are imprisoned and released without being brought to trial. There is probably at least a *prima facie* case against such persons, whereas many of the Lerwick Staff could not possibly have had anything to do with the alleged offence and no attempt was made to ascertain whether there was any evidence or *prima facie* case against them."

He concluded: "It is not the practice of the Post Office to make a formal record until the delinquent has been adjudged guilty. In this instance it became obvious at an early stage in the investigation that the charge could not be substantiated, and there is therefore no record of the case in the Lerwick Misconduct Book."

---

3   Letter and draft letter – NAS, HH31/17.
4   Murray to Dodds – NAS, HH31/17.

The Prison Commission for Scotland however continued to assert that there was no difference between the arrest and release of the Lerwick Post Office Staff and other individuals in the same situation.[5]

"It is a mistake to suppose that the Lerwick staff of the Post Office are the only people who have been lodged in prison against whom the charges made were without foundation," stated Mr Devon.

Sir James, again writing to Mr Murray, suggests adding a note saying: "All the above named men were released at the instance of the Admiralty who expressed themselves satisfied that the charges against them were wholly unfounded."[6] This would be added immediately if it met with the Postmaster General's approval.

He then added: "In view of what you say about entries in the Post Office Misconduct Book I should like to emphasise the fact that the Register in question is simply a daily record which the Governor is required to keep of persons for whose reception and discharge he is responsible. The fact that the name of a person appears there does not prove that such person has been guilty of any contravention of the law, unless his conviction for some offence is recorded. The register is thus hardly comparable with the Post Office 'Black Book'".

"Dear Sir James Dodds," replied Murray, "I am much obliged for your letter of yesterday.[7] I recognise the difficulty of going beyond the note which you suggest, which may to some extent mitigate the resentment of the Post Office staff, and I shall be grateful if you would have it inserted in the Prison Records."

On 13th October Mr Devon wrote the following letter to Sir James: "The Warder in charge of Lerwick Prison intimates that the following note has been inserted in the Criminal Register after the names of the Post Office officials.[8]

"'All the above-named men were released at the instance of the Admiralty who expressed themselves satisfied that the charges against them were wholly unfounded.'

"I trust this will close the incident."

Sir James copied the information, using much the same terms, to Mr Murray.[9] At the same time he replied to Mr Devon saying that he had written to Mr Murray telling him that the note had been added. In conclusion he expressed the hope that "we have heard the last of a troublesome question. With many thanks for your co-operation in getting the matter settled."

5   Letter from Devon to Gascoigne at GPO – NAS, HH31/17.
6   Dodds to Murray at GPO – NAS, HH31/17.
7   Murray to Dodds – NAS, HH31/17.
8   Devon to Dodds – NAS, HH31/17.
9   Letter 8th October, 1915 – NAS, HH31/17.

Mr Murray's reply was brief.[10] "Thanks for your letter. I hope the Lerwick incident may now be regarded as closed."

On 1st November 1915 a telegram arrived for the staff at Lerwick Post Office. It came from Mr Macmaster and contained greetings to the staff on the anniversary of the arrest.[11]

10   19th October, 1915 – NAS, HH31/17.
11   Letter from Mr Macmaster to George Manson, dated 4th April, 1958.

CHAPTER 22

Evans

LT COL EVANS' summary arrest of the Post Office staff had not enhanced the esteem in which he was held.

He had endeavoured to make his presence felt from the moment of his arrival in Shetland. His habit of barking "I'm waiting" in a southern English accent at any of the Naval Reserve who omitted to salute him in the street did nothing to endear him to the servicemen or the population of Lerwick. His English seemed as foreign to the Shetlanders as no doubt their dialect seemed to him. They regarded him as a pompous idiot. For his part he probably regarded the Shetlanders as 'natives', influenced by his birth and upbringing in North-western India in the late nineteenth century.

His posting to Shetland when war was imminent owed more to his experience of intelligence-gathering than to his familiarity with command, as he had spent much of his service up to that time in gathering information on various topics, mainly in the far east. He had received commendations for these reports and it seems likely that he was selected to go to Shetland on the basis of these. Winston Churchill had laid specific emphasis on organising an intelligence network in Shetland because of the perceived threat of disloyalty among the populace.

From the evidence of his career record[1] it would seem that his superiors did not consider that being in command of troops was his strong point. Since his father was a colonel the army would have been an automatic choice for him but perhaps it was not the right one.

The first entries in his career record are very favourable but there is then a curious incident. He is posted to the Army Service Corps but it is a very short posting. Just a

---

[1]   Career information on Evans – National Archives (Kew), ADM 196/62.

year later there is an entry reading "The reports of the General Officer Commanding Aldershot on Lieut. Evans not being entirely satisfactory he does not desire to retain his services in the Army Service Corps for a longer period. Ordered he rejoin his Divisional Headquarters, Chatham."

Despite continuing favourable reports in his record – "a very good and able officer" – when he is finally posted as a marine officer aboard ship, the length of time he spends on each ship seems remarkably short. At one point he is ordered to leave his ship and return overland from Trieste. He was then sent to Plymouth for two years. Eventually he was sent to HMS *Tamar*, the shore station at Hong Kong and from there he sent intelligence reports on the situation in China and the German South Pacific Islands.

On his return he was posted to Portsmouth and stayed there for two years until he was sent to Shetland to command the local Royal Naval Reserve.

The arrest of the Lerwick Post Office staff and their subsequent release seem not to have affected Evans' immediate position in Shetland. In January 1915 he was designated Competent Naval Authority, Shetlands. The outcry over the arrest and the fact that someone had made a huge blunder was obviously not attributed to him by his superiors. The fact that he was getting the blame in Lerwick and that relations

An RNR training group in the grounds of Fort Charlotte in 1915 with Lieutenant Arthur Nicolson from Fetlar and Col Evans in front.

Photo: A Abernethy, Shetland Museum and Archives Photo Library

between the local population and the military were at an all-time low had not penetrated to those in command further south. It was, however, all too apparent to Post Office headquarters and had resulted in the transfer of the postmaster.

It was wartime and therefore the first objective of the authorities was to ensure unity and to avoid criticism of those in command.

The attitude of the GPO however contrasts sharply with that of the Prison Commissioners. Where the Post Office tends to regard the stance taken by the postmaster as understandable but a nuisance and removes him from the scene, the Prison Service, in particular Mr Crombie, regards Evans' conduct as high-handed to say the least, and unreasonable.

There is no record of Evans' thoughts on the subject but it seems from his subsequent conduct that he did not consider that he had acted improperly in any way. He continued with his draconian methods of discipline.

On Sunday, 5th September, 1915, Evans led a church parade of the local Royal Naval Reserve troops.[2] Seaman Balfour was astounded, on their return to Fort Charlotte, to be accused of chewing tobacco during the service and spitting on the church floor.

"I don't chew tobacco," he thought. "I don't even smoke. It wasn't me. What is he on about?"

Evans looked up Balfour's name in the register and found that he was over eighteen years of age and could not therefore be birched.

"I cannot order you to be birched for this offence," he said to Balfour, who looked at him in amazement. "So I will give you the option of seven days' detention in the cells or six strokes with the lash."

Seaman Balfour could not believe it. He had not committed any offence but quite obviously that was not going to weigh with Evans. He knew that seven days in the cells would be a dreadful ordeal, if indeed he survived it; so six strokes with the lash seemed the lesser of two evils. He opted for that. He was stripped, laid across a gun on the parade square of Fort Charlotte and duly flogged.

News of this is a small place like Lerwick could not of course hope to be kept secret. The RNR servicemen told their families and word spread. There was nothing to be done about it, but it did not add to Evans' popularity.

Worse was to follow. On 2nd October in the early morning Charles Sutherland died in a cell at Fort Charlotte. He had been accused of a breach of naval discipline and sentenced to two days' in the cells. He emphatically denied that he had committed the offence and indeed there was no evidence to prove that he was guilty

---

2   National Archives – ADM 12/1545B; code 78.1 and code 78.2.

but this did not help him. He was also ordered to break road metal and he was expected to do this on just 1 lb. of bread each day to eat and water to drink.

The weather was bad, cold and windy, and the cell was draughty. There was no heating of any kind. He was not supplied with warm clothing. On the morning of the second he was found dead. This time people demanded action.

In the House of Commons on 20th October Cathcart Wason asked the First Lord of the Admiralty[3] if it had been reported to him that a man named Charles Sutherland, belonging to the Shetland section, Royal Naval Reserve, had died in a cell at Fort Charlotte, Lerwick, at 6 am on the 2nd instant. He recounted the circumstances surrounding the death and asked if the First Lord had any information on the subject. He asked also if he was aware that the officer in charge of the troops had ordered another member of the Shetland RNR to be flogged for an offence of which he was certainly not guilty. He ended by asking if the First Lord would state how he proposed to deal with the officer responsible for the execution of these sentences.

Dr Macnamara, replying for the First Lord, said that no information had reached the Admiralty respecting either of the cases mentioned. Reports, however, had been called for.

In this he spoke no less than the truth. Reports were urgently called for and the results of the enquiries duly noted.[4]

> "Death in prison at Lerwick of C. Sutherland, Shetland R.N.R., irregularly punished by Col HC Evans RM, Commanding troops in Shetland. Court of enquiry. Col Evans relieved of command. Severe displeasure. As to irregular use of Fort Charlotte as detention quarters. Parliamentary questions."
>
> "Caning of Seaman Balfour RNR, although over 18, irregularly punished by Col HC Evans RM, commanding troops in Shetland. Court of enquiry. Col Evans relieved of command. Severe displeasure. Irregular confinement of men in cells at Fort Charlotte for detention. Parliamentary questions."

Evans was duly relieved of command very swiftly and left Lerwick on 28th November, a little over a year after his arrest of the Post Office staff. He returned to Portsmouth and thereafter his career reports read 'Unfavourable'. He applied several times for promotion to colonel, perhaps wishing to emulate his father. Each time he was refused and a note added at the foot of his career record reads: "Before any future promotion of this officer is considered reference should be made to Papers C.B. 864."

---

3   Hansard – 20th October, 1915.
4   As Footnote No.2 – transcript.

In a curious footnote to the fate of Charles Sutherland, his death was not recorded until after Evans had left Shetland. He is registered as having died on 2nd October 1915 in a detention cell in Fort Charlotte, Lerwick. His usual address is given as Tourie, Haroldswick, Unst and his occupation as fisherman and RNR reservist and he was a married man. The cause of death is recorded as 'fatigue and exposure to cold'. The certificate, however, is dated 13th December and the informant is none other than the Procurator Fiscal, J. Kirkland Galloway.

CHAPTER 23

1916 to 1921

MR MACMASTER again sent a telegram to the staff at Lerwick Post Office on 1st November 1916, on the second anniversary of the arrest. He still felt angry towards Post Office headquarters and he had in no way forgotten his former staff although he was not in a position at that time to help them fight their cause.

However, Cathcart Wason continued to campaign on behalf of the Post Office staff. He wrote once more to the Postmaster General on 17th June 1917 asking for the case to be reopened. Mr Albert Illingworth had by now replaced Hobhouse but the response from the GPO was the same, as revealed by this internal memo to the Postmaster General:[1]

"It is clearly out of the question to reopen the matter; and I submit that Mr. Cathcart Wason be answered as follows:-

"I have looked into the facts of the incident at Lerwick about which you wrote me on the 17th instant.

"I find that the circumstances were repeatedly considered by my predecessors who were of the opinion that the matter had been settled in as satisfactory a manner as was practicable, and declined to reopen the question in response to requests from the Staff. I entirely concur in this view, and regret therefore that I am unable to take any steps in the direction suggested."

On 1st November 1917 another telegram was received by the staff at Lerwick from Mr Macmaster. Another anniversary was remembered.

1918 saw the end of the war at last. Few of the Royal Naval Reserve raised by Evans had survived to see it. Evans himself had spent the years after leaving Lerwick in Portsmouth and retired in April 1918, having seen no active service.

---

1   Memo, June 1917 – The British Postal Museum & Archive.

Towards the end of 1918 Macmaster applied for promotion to Kilmarnock Post Office.[2] He gave as his reason for leaving Wellingborough and seeking promotion: "I have been long enough here." He still felt anger towards headquarters and was in no mood for finesse at his interview. He sent his anniversary telegram as usual to the Lerwick staff and awaited the results of his interview. He thought if he was refused the posting that he would know how he was regarded at headquarters, but he was given the promotion. Again he was asked if he would take the compensation offered by the Admiralty and again he refused it, in no uncertain and scarcely polite terms.

At the end of 1918 Zetland County Council entered the lists. At a meeting of the council on 19th December the following minute was recorded:[3]

An extract from a council minute including the demand for a public apology.

National Archives of Scotland

> 25478/4458
>
> **COUNTY OF ZETLAND.**
>
> Certified Excerpt from Minutes of Meeting of the County Council of Zetland, held at Lerwick on the 19th December, 1918.
>
> "Mr. Mouat thereafter referred to the arrest, at the early stages of the war, of the Postmaster of Lerwick and the whole Post Office Staff, and their confinement for some days in Lerwick Prison. He said it was a disgrace to the Islands, and although the people in Shetland knew it was a gross mistake, it was not generally known, and even in Canada and the United States it was not understood the Authorities were in error. Any one who saw these loyal citizens being marched up, under an armed escort, to the Prison, on a Sunday forenoon, could not but feel indignant; and he moved that the County Council demand and press for a public apology from the Authorities, and an admission that they were in the wrong; and also for an explanation for their wrongous action, which was unanimously agreed to. The Clerk was instructed to communicate this resolution to the Admiralty, the Prime Minister, the Secretary for Scotland, and the Member for the County."
>
> A correct excerpt, certified by.
>
> County Clerk.

---

2   Macmaster's correspondence with George Manson.
3   Excerpt from minutes – NAS, HH31/17.

"Mr Mouat thereafter referred to the arrest, at the early stages of the war, of the Postmaster of Lerwick and the whole Post Office Staff, and their confinement for some days in Lerwick Prison. He said it was a disgrace to the Islands, and although the people in Shetland knew that it was a gross mistake, it was not generally known, and even in Canada and the United States it was not understood the Authorities were in error. Any one who saw these loyal citizens being marched up, under an armed escort, to the Prison, on a Sunday forenoon (sic), could not but feel indignant; and he moved that the County Council demand and press for a public apology from the Authorities, and an admission that they were in the wrong; and also for an explanation for their wrongous action, which was unanimously agreed to. The Clerk was instructed to communicate this resolution to the Admiralty, the Prime Minister, the Secretary for Scotland, and the Member for the County."

Predictably this request also fell on deaf ears.

As Cathcart Wason had had no success, and Zetland County Council had failed also to gain redress for the staff, they turned to the National Joint Committee of Post Office Associations for help. The committee duly took up their case and wrote to the Postmaster General in March 1919. The response in April was once more negative.[4]

"Sir,
    Lerwick. Arrest of Post Office Staff in 1914.
"In reply to your letter of the 14th ultimo, I am directed by the Postmaster General to say that the circumstances in connexion with the incident at Lerwick in November 1914 were repeatedly considered by his predecessors, who were of the opinion that the matter could not profitably be reopened. Mr. Illingworth concurs in this view and regrets that he cannot see his way to take any steps in the direction suggested.
    "I am to add that no record of the arrest was made in the Post Office Conduct Records and that, as regards the entry in the Prison Books, a note was made that "All the above named men were released at the instance of the Admiralty who expressed themselves satisfied that the charges against them were wholly unfounded.""

Comparing the Post Office letter of June 1917 and the letter of April 1919 one cannot escape the similarities. The conclusion must be that the writer had looked up the file, copied the last relevant letter and added a bit here and there.

There the matter seems to rest. None of the attempts made to reopen the case and to obtain an explanation and apology met with any success. There remained the question of the compensation.

Mr Macmaster had steadfastly refused to accept any compensation, regarding it as an insult. However he put no pressure on the Lerwick Staff to accept or refuse, considering it a matter for each individual to resolve for himself. No-one knew who had accepted and who had refused. Another internal memo to the Postmaster General, however, sheds some light on this.[5]

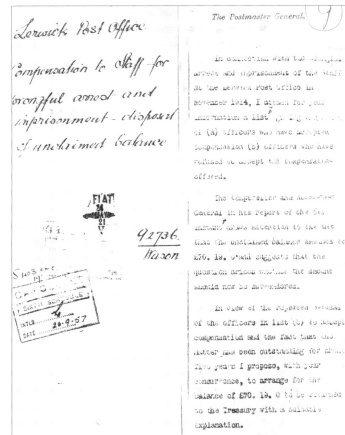

Details of the sum left over after the repeated refusal of some staff to accept compensation.

5   The British Postal Museum & Archive.

"In connection with the wrongful arrest and imprisonment of the Staff at the Lerwick Post Office in November 1914, I attach for your information a list of (a) officers who have accepted compensation (b) officers who have refused to accept the compensation offered.

"The Comptroller and Accountant General in his report of the 5th instant draws attention to the fact that the unclaimed balance amounts to £70. 19s. 0 and suggests that the question arises whether the amount should now be surrendered.

"In view of the repeated refusal of the officers in list (b) to accept compensation and the fact that the matter has been outstanding for about five years I propose, with your concurrence, to arrange for the balance of £70. 19. 0 to be returned to the Treasury with a suitable explanation."

What suitable explanation could there be? None, it is certain, that would be palatable to the Admiralty or to Government. As the original sum of money offered for compensation was £104. 11s. it is obvious that only a small minority of the staff had taken the money, those probably in most need possibly, though some indeed took it only to hand it over immediately to the local Gilbert Bain Hospital.

Thus ended the staff's campaign for redress, for an explanation and an apology, for an acknowledgment of the fact that they had been wrongfully arrested and that their names should never have been recorded in a criminal register. This was something which they felt very strongly about and it is ironic that their determined effort to have their names removed from the register should result in theirs being the only names from that period still on record. In order to ascertain how best to remove their names, copies were made of the pages from the register containing them and sent to the Prison Commission in Edinburgh. These copies are the only remaining records from that period at Lerwick, as the register itself has been lost.

CHAPTER 24

Mr Macmaster

IN SHARP CONTRAST to the character and actions of Evans, James Macmaster showed an integrity and courage which endeared him to his staff. Where Evans demanded loyalty and obedience from his troops, Macmaster's actions commanded loyalty and admiration from his staff.

He did not need to share a prison cell with them. He was offered accommodation on the yacht *Shemara* but refused, preferring to be with his staff. In later years he admitted that that might have been a mistake if any one of the staff had been found guilty, but he felt he knew them so well and could judge that none of them would commit an act of espionage.

His presence in the Lerwick prison certainly had a great effect on the morale of the men. When he joined them about half an hour after they had been marched through the door, their spirits lifted. What had seemed like a nightmare began to take on the aspect of a joke to some, a holiday, a break from routine. To the postmaster and overseers it was no joke. Macmaster's presence among them, however, helped enormously. With him there, they presented a united front. His obvious trust in his staff, by staying there with them, put a great deal of pressure on the authorities. If he had accepted Commander Startin's offer, and let his staff go to prison without him, it would have been much easier for the Admiralty to make an example of one or more of them, guilty or not. This became impossible once the postmaster joined them.

It is part of his character that he would refuse, in a polite and unobtrusive manner, to co-operate with those in authority. He would not ask his wife to bring in bedding from home. He used prison blankets. He wanted to eat nothing but prison food but the warder managed to persuade him otherwise. When asked for the keys of the safe, he would not hand them over without authorisation from headquarters and it is typical of him that he would put as his address 'Cell 1, H.M.Prison, Lerwick' on a telegram to Post Office headquarters.

He led the campaign for an explanation and an apology on their release from prison and he did so with such forcefulness that the Post Office moved him out of Lerwick to stop his influence over the staff. It did not have the desired effect, however, as he had set an example which the rest of them were keen to follow.

The agitation continued. Macmaster had no idea that he had been removed to separate him from the staff. He accepted that it was promotion of a kind and continued after that to apply for other posts. From Lerwick he went to Wellingborough and from there to Kilmarnock. From there he went to Greenock, then to Perth and finally to Dundee. He had thought perhaps that his stance at Lerwick might have harmed his chances of promotion, but in fact it seemed to have helped him as he felt that merit alone would not have taken him so far. In this he is undoubtedly wrong.

The qualities of leadership and loyalty to his staff that he showed in Lerwick are inestimable. These alone would have ensured his promotion, but it is also possible that those in authority in the Post Office felt a little guilty at their lack of support at the time when it was needed most.

He continued to send a telegram from Wellingborough for some years but eventually stopped as he thought it was unfair to his successor to carry on with it. His influence lingered for much longer as the staff continued to campaign for an explanation, for a public apology and for their names to be removed from the criminal register, from a record in which they should never have been entered.

Conclusion

SHETLANDERS have long served in the Royal Navy. There were Shetlanders at Trafalgar, some even on board the *Victory*.

It is strange therefore to see the loyalty of the Shetlanders questioned, as it was by the Admiralty and the First Lord of the Admiralty, Winston Churchill. The first mention of this is recorded in a minute from Churchill to Rear-Admiral Bethell, Director of Naval Intelligence. Churchill is asking for advice about setting up a wireless station in Shetland, and perhaps a small torpedo-boat base. He then goes on to inquire about German influence in the Islands. Bethell replies that there would be no real necessity for a wireless station as Shetland would be the wartime base for the 7th Cruiser Squadron and he adds that German influence is not very marked in the islands and there had been very few German ships there since 1904.

Despite this reassurance from Bethell, Churchill persists in putting forward the idea of German influence in Shetland. In all probability he had read the scathing editorial in *The Shetland Times*, written when the Navy had sent just four ships in response to a request for a show of strength from Britain. It would seem likely that he misunderstood the Shetland sense of irony and assumed that they thought the Germans superior. However, in view of the fact that he was trying to reinforce the defences in the north and to persuade the government to retain the Territorial Forces it would seem possible that he was using the idea of Shetland disloyalty as a lever for his own ends.

Churchill again brought up the subject of German influence in Shetland at meetings of the Committee for Imperial Defence in 1912. The following year finds him cruising on the Admiralty yacht along with Prime Minister Asquith round the north of Scotland. They visit Scapa Flow and then head straight for the Western Isles. Churchill makes no attempt to visit Shetland and see for himself whether the natives are friendly or not.

As he was presumably inspecting the defences at Scapa Flow and naval installations on the West coast of Scotland, it is difficult to understand why he did not include Shetland in his itinerary if he had any real doubts about the loyalty of the Shetlanders. This, I feel, reinforces the idea that he was using the idea of disloyalty in Shetland for political reasons. He wanted to build up defences in the north of Britain and probably considered that the Defence Committee would be more receptive to his proposals if they thought there was a threat to security from the local population.

Whatever his reasons for sowing doubt about Shetland's loyalty, the damage had been done and the rumours persisted, right up to the beginning of the War, to the extent that the Admiralty, in the person of Vice-Admiral Sir George Warrender, sends a signal to the Fleet warning them that the Germans might have a submarine base in Shetland and that some Shetlanders are suspected of being in sympathy with the enemy. These doubts can stem only from Winston Churchill's persistence in putting them forward. There can be no other reason. In the Navy itself, many refused to believe in the rumours.

Among the Admiralty hierarchy in Scapa Flow, however, it is likely that some were predisposed, because of Admiral Warrender's signal, to think that there might be spies in Shetland, especially as spy stories seemed to form the chief topic in the newspapers. Any letter which was even vaguely suspicious would be immediately seized upon and all letters coming from Shetland would be scrutinised carefully.

The missing letter

A THREAD running through all of the accounts of the arrest of the Post Office staff has been speculation on the nature of the letter which caused it. There are several versions of this. My mother's version was that the letter went missing. Addressed to Swarbacks Minn in Shetland, it ended up at Swanbister in Orkney. Another version has it turning up in a seemingly empty mailbag in the Lerwick Post Office after the release of the staff. Mr Macmaster would seem to corroborate this, as he returned a letter found in a seemingly empty mailbag to Swarbacks Minn in person. Both of these versions deny that it was important; it was just a list of stores.

It appears, however, from a study of the archive documents, that these accounts are wrong. There was no missing letter.

Till now it has been assumed that it was mail arriving in Shetland that caused the trouble. I feel it is much more likely that it was mail sent from Shetland, from Swarbacks Minn to Scapa Flow. Navy officials at Scapa Flow would be on the lookout for anything suspicious coming from Shetland after Admiral Warrender's signal. Perhaps a crumpled envelope would be enough to merit their attention. The speed with which it reached London suggests that it was sent from Scapa Flow directly.

If this is the case, then Mr Macmaster's trip in person to Swarbacks Minn with an unimportant letter must have puzzled the officials there.

In an informal note, hand-written on Admiralty paper on 7th November 1914, the day on which the staff were released, it is clear that the suspicious letter was already in the hands of the Admiralty in London.

J M Evans wrote from the Admiralty to Mr Smith at the office of the Secretary for Scotland notifying him that they had sent a telegram to the Vice-Admiral instructing him to release the men *'unless the investigation showed that any individual was guilty'*. This note acknowledges that the inquiry had not shed any light on the subject and admits that there was no reason for suspecting a large number of tampering with the mail – *'if indeed any have'*. It adds that the inquiry has not been very exhaustive and reveals that *'some of the opened covers'* were there.

Thus, there was no missing letter; just a suspicious one which looked as if it had been tampered with. This letter must have been forwarded from Scapa Flow to the Admiralty in London. We can assume, therefore, that it was one *received* by the Naval authorities at Scapa Flow and not one which had been sent by them.

This informal note also contains a tacit admission, on the part of the Admiralty, that very few, *if any*, of the men should have been arrested and put in jail. In the statement, *'There is no reason for suspecting that any large number of the staff have been guilty of tampering with the letter – if indeed any have'* there is a clear indication that the Admiralty knew they had done the wrong thing. It was to take many months, however, before any admission of this kind was made to those who had suffered most – the staff of the Lerwick Post Office.

The Admiralty was of the opinion that the two outer covers had been steamed open and the seal on the innermost had been slit carefully. When the letter was submitted for examination by Post Office experts, they were quite clear in their conclusions. An internal memo to the Postmaster General states that *'the suspicion of the Admiralty rested on the case of one letter alone'* and that the officers of the Investigative Branch of the Post Office were of the opinion that the letter *'had not been tampered with at all'*.

The instructions for the arrest and questioning of the Post Office staff therefore must have originated in London. It is doubtful that the intention was to throw the whole lot in jail, as it was extremely unlikely that all of them would have been involved in tampering with one letter. It is unlikely too that the Admiralty expected that all of them would be detained for six days and nonsensical to suppose that the Admiralty wanted them to be held in jail without being questioned.

It was, however, a huge mistake to entrust a commission of this kind to such an erratic disciplinarian as Lt Col Evans. I am sure that his actions took the Admiralty by surprise and the subsequent uproar raised by the population, the sheriffs, the Scottish Office, the Prison Commissioners, the newspapers and the MP for Orkney and

Shetland caused acute embarrassment. This, coupled with the fact that the Post Office experts stated that the letter had not been tampered with, must be the reason for the fact that none of the staff were ever questioned and that they were released without explanation.

Aftermath

THE STAFF on their release felt justifiably incensed. They had been thrown into jail without having been explicitly accused of anything. They had never been questioned and therefore they had had no chance of exonerating themselves. They had been forced to support themselves, or their families had, while in jail. They had been released without explanation either for the arrest or discharge.

When they returned to work they found the Post Office reluctant to pay their wages for the time they had been locked up. There was no sign of an apology from the Admiralty for the indignity they had had to suffer. And they were innocent.

It is no wonder that such wholesale incarceration should have caused the furore that it did. Sir James Dodds' allusion to the Zabern affair in his letter to Lamb at Westminster shows clearly that he at least thought the situation had been badly handled. The army stationed at Zabern in Alsace had made a local incident into a national confrontation. One of the army officers had called the Zabern inhabitants 'Wackos' – a huge insult. The people naturally protested against this. The officer treated this protest as a rebellion and threw many into jail, including the mayor of the town and a judge.

By the time that the German Parliament heard about it the damage had been done and Alsace, which had been annexed by Germany, was threatening to rejoin France. This was in 1913 when relations with France were at a low ebb anyway. It was resolved in a fashion when that particular officer was sent elsewhere but the local people were not completely satisfied. It was the attitude of those in command which rankled most.

It is probable that Sir James detected something of that attitude in the wholesale arrest of the Post Office staff; indeed it seems likely that he was right. Lt Col Evans's upbringing in India and his posting to the Far East would have inculcated in him an attitude that the local population was somehow inferior and could be treated with, if not contempt, condescension. He would not have thought that he had to consider their feelings on the subject at all.

This attitude was not confined to Evans. The Admiralty's answer to the staff's false imprisonment seems to have been to throw money at them. They offered compensation. In this they showed a complete misunderstanding of the men they were dealing with. It was an extremely patronising and insulting thing to do, to try and fob them off with what might be called a bribe. The government also seemed to feel a little uncomfortable about this. It is noticeable that in agreeing to pay compensation they took care that it came from a fund that required no notification to Parliament and would thus incur no questions in the House. This offer was treated with the contempt it deserved. Very few of the staff took the money.

This subject also has been embellished over the years. My grandfather, Hug Tait, did not take the compensation offered, but my mother said that some men did, only to hand it over to the Gilbert Bain Hospital in Lerwick. The same story is echoed in other accounts to the extent that there is no doubt that this is what happened in many cases

The Admiralty finally apologised, but not in a public statement. A notice was sent to be displayed in the Post Office and individuals were given letters of apology. Therefore there was still widespread ignorance in places other than Shetland as to whether the staff were spies or not. In the United States and Canada there were many Shetland associations and relatives writing home from there told of their dismay to learn of spies in Shetland from American papers. There is no doubt that a public statement should have been issued, but it was wartime. When the campaign for an apology continued after the war, the authorities dismissed it again.

Relations between the local population and the military were strained, to say the least, after the arrest. The Shetlanders blamed Lt Col Evans for most of it but the Admiralty seem not to have taken this view. Instead of censure he remained Officer in charge of Troops, Shetland. It was not until the death of Charles Sutherland that the Admiralty began to look askance at him. This incident was the reason for him being first censured and then relieved of his command. For the most part people considered that he had been removed because of his handling of the arrest, but the Admiralty could not remove him for that, as they had ordered him to detain the staff in the first place. That he misinterpreted his orders was neither here nor there.

The fact that their names had been recorded in the Criminal Register, however, was the subject that infuriated the staff most. They demanded the removal of their names but although the Prison Commissioners were sympathetic they would not agree to the Register being altered. Once again we see the same attitude resurfacing. Those in authority, in government, could not understand why the staff was making such a fuss. Their names were there, yes, but also the record that they had been released on the authority of the Admiralty with no charge against them. They were in the same position as anyone arrested and released without charge. But they were not. None of them should have been arrested. It was a blunder. Making noises about others having been detained and released without charge could not alter that fact and could not relieve the sense of humiliation that the arrest had left with them.

The authorities completely failed to grasp that it was not just the shame of having their name on the register. It was not just because they were innocent. It was a matter of justice, of the right and proper course of action on the part of government.

It should have been expected that the General Post Office gave every support to their employees, however remote. It does seem, however, that the GPO was deficient in this respect. Mr Macmaster complained of their attitude also. He thought they showed a distinct lack of interest, especially in the Postmaster General's reply to Cathcart Wason. Subsequent memos and letters from the GPO bear this out. In spite of being requested by the National Joint Committee of Post Office Associations to reopen the subject of the wrongful arrest, the GPO refused to do so, even after the war when it would have been less embarrassing for the government.

There is, however, one letter, written on 14th September 1915 from the General Post Office to Sir James Dodds, Undersecretary for Scotland, which does acknowledge that the case of the Lerwick Post Office staff did differ from that of other persons imprisoned and released without trial.

Mr Murray wrote that 'There is probably at least a prima facie case against such persons, whereas many of the Lerwick staff could not possibly have had anything to do with the alleged offence and no attempt was made to ascertain whether there was any evidence or prima facie case against them.' He added that no record of the arrest had been entered in the Post Office Misconduct Book 'as it became obvious at an early stage in the investigation that the charge could not be substantiated'.

This opinion did not seem to carry any weight with Sir James Dodds. He replied, majestically: 'In view of what you say about entries in the Post Office Misconduct Book I should like to emphasise the fact that the Register in question is simply a daily record which the Governor is required to keep of persons for whose reception and discharge he is responsible. The fact that the name of a person appears there does not prove that such person has been guilty of any contravention of the law, unless his conviction for some offence is recorded. The Register is thus hardly comparable with the Post Office "Black Book".' Their names were not removed from the Register.

If the staff had not been so persistent in trying to remove their names from the Register there would now be no record, no proof that they had ever been arrested. The records for Lerwick Prison for that period have been lost. It is only because of their fight to have their names erased from the Register that those pages have survived. They were copied so that the Prison Commission could best decide how to erase them from the book, and so found their way into the Scottish National Archives. The irony of this would have been lost on my grandfather. He would not have seen the joke.

My grandfather left Lerwick reluctantly in 1926. He could not get promotion to head postmaster in Lerwick because he belonged there so he went to Kirkwall, in Orkney. While he was there he managed, with the help of the postmaster at Inverness, to set up the first internal airmail service in Britain. Not bad for a jailbird.

Names of those in the photograph as recalled by James Williamson on 14 August 1979, at the age of 88. Those names in bold were members of staff who were jailed the following year.

1 James J Robertson (senior postman); 2 Andrew B Jamieson; 3 Alexander Sandison; *4 William A Thomson;* 5 David J J Tait; *6 Robert Mackay; 7 George W Manson; 8 Joseph P Sutherland;* 9 James Williamson; 10 Peter Robertson (son of No.1 above); 11 Gilbert kay; *12 Charles M Arthur*; 13 James J Tait (Hug);* 14 James Leiper (head postmaster); *15 William Stout;* 16 William Fraser (from Kingston-on-Spey); *17 John S Shewan; 18 William Spanswick (office caretaker);* 19 Magnus Murray; *20 Thomas Pottinger;* 21 R Shepherd (from Inverness); *22 William H Arthur*;* 23 John W. Manson; *24 William G Grant; 25 Robert B Blance; 26 Andrew P Hawick;* 27 A R M Mathewson; 28 Jack Slade (from Fowey, Cornwall); 29 James Pyper; *30 John M Arthur*; 31 Robert Paton; 32 Alfred Hay;* 33 John Gray (from Aberdeenshire).   * These three were brothers.

Appendix II

THE FOLLOWING correspondence is from James Macmaster to George Manson several years after the incident at Lerwick Post Office.

Little Garth
Ridgeway
Boars Hill
Oxford
24th January 1957

Dear Mr Manson

Very many thanks for granting me the privilege of reading your account of the Naval and Military manoeuvres at Lerwick on 1st Nov. 1914. I found it very interesting and in it you told me of happenings of which I was not fully aware hitherto. Your sense of humour has not faded with the passing of the years.

There are one or two items in your story which do not quite tally with my recollections, but I may well be wrong as memory plays us all strange tricks. I think, for instance, that the arrest took place in the afternoon. Again, I was only twice outside the prison walls during the six days. The first occasion was when I went to the Post Office to issue a supply of stamps, etc. for public use, and the second when I was allowed out to meet officials from P.O.H.Q. I notice, too, that you promote me to Dundee as if I went there direct from Lerwick while, actually, it too me 13 years to get there, stopping off – as Americans would say – at Wellingborough, Kilmarnock, Greenock and Perth. To get to Dundee was a long way to go – like Tipperary.

I would like, too, to make other things clearer. First of all it is well you should know that I had no foreknowledge of the happenings at Lerwick on 1st Nov. 1914 and was as much bewildered by them as you must have been. I mention this because on the day before the event an official (telegraphic) inquiry reached me asking what staff was required at Lerwick. There was no need of staff and I said so in replying. It is clear this inquiry indicated that P.O.H.Q. was aware of what was about to happen and may have thought that I was too, but this was not so.

When you were marched away from the P.O. I had no idea of your destination. As for me I was left in the custody of a Naval officer who invited me to accompany him aboard one of H.M. ships in the harbour. But I said that I wished first of all to see where the staff had gone to and to this he made no demur. He walked up the lane opposite the P.O. to my house and then on to the Prison. I thought I might find you at the Town Hall or, peradventure, at Fort Charlotte and was taken aback and annoyed at the Prison where, I quickly told my escort, I intended to stay. He made no objection. I joined up with you within 30 minutes of your arrest. We were all in the show and for better or worse it seemed to me only proper we should remain together. There are some who might say it was a rash decision but I have never regretted it. If there had been a sinner amongst us I fear my action would not have met with official approval and what might have happened is anybody's guess.

I need not recount all the happenings in prison as you have done this admirably and with imagination. On, I think, the day after arrest I was asked to hand over the keys of the safes, etc., but declined to do so unless instructed by P.O.H.Q. What happened outside the prison after my refusal I don't know but later I was instructed by Telegraph to proceed to the Post Office – if required under escort – and hand over supplies. In acknowledging this instruction I gave my address as – Cell No. 1, H. M. Prison Lerwick just to give P.O.H.Q. a jolt. I hope it did.

On the day of our release two H.Q. staff called to see me at my house and, much to my astonishment, suggested that we resume duty forthwith but I was in no mood to do so until affairs had been fully cleared up. No reasons or apologies for the arrest were forthcoming. In any case, I said, the staff would have to be consulted and so I invited some members to come to see me at my house. As they seemed to favour a return to duty I fell in with their views and so we all went back to the office on the following Monday.

The Naval Auths. took a long time (4 months) before absolving us from blame and in the interval I protested about the delay, which was both disturbing and inexcusable. When the announcement was made in the House of Commons I was on leave and in the South of England and I remember telegraphing to Lerwick saying that it did not satisfy me.

I disliked the attitude of the PMG who seemed to me to show indifference as if the matter hardly concerned his Department. I gave him a lead by recommending that two of the Lerwick staff should be promoted and all others awarded a special increment. It was also suggested that o/c Troops had outstayed his welcome in Shetland and might well be transferred elsewhere.

As a personal matter I would like to say that I never at any time while at Lerwick applied for promotion. I was invited to go to Wellingborough which was definitely not promotion, merely a transfer. True, the salary at W. was £10 more but on the whole I was £50 out of pocket and in those days £50 was a lot of money. Later I was to go to Kilmarnock, Greenock and Perth and finally Dundee.

At Wellingborough, I may mention, I applied for leave to enlist in the Army but permission was refused.

I left Lerwick somewhat under a cloud – uncertain of the future.

I refused the Admiralty's donation and never got to know what our arrest was all about.

I liked Shetland and its people and regret my stay was so short.

Your further news is awaited with great interest

With kindest regards

Yours faithfully,

J Macmaster

[There is a pencil note at the end of the letter saying that it is not of course intended for publication.]

Memo regarding the Swarback Minn incident on Monday 9th Nov. 1914.

When the Lerwick Post Office staff resumed duty on Mon. 9 Nov. 1914 they found a good deal needing to be cleared up. There were, for instance, quite a lot of empty mail bags which had all to be turned inside out. In one of them, returned as empty from the Naval ships at Swarback Minn, a small canvas mail bag was found. It was addressed to the Commanding Officer and the seal was unbroken. The bag was handed to the Postmaster who gave it to the Post Office officers from H.Q. then at Lerwick. These officers and the Postmaster proceeded to Swarbacks Minn and went on board the Flag ship where they saw the C.O. and handed over the bag to him at the same time making him aware of the circumstances in which it had been found. He opened the bag and said the contents were not of importance. He made suitable apology for the trouble caused by the carelessness of his officers.

[This memo is part of the letter of 24th January 1957.]

Little Garth
Boar's Hill
Oxford
1st Nov. 1957

Dear Mr Manson,

What a pleasure it was to hear your voice again after the passage of so many years – 43 of them. Our talk was much too short and I had scarcely time to say much more than how-do-you-do and good-bye. Many thanks for calling me on a very memorable anniversary. Thank those who sent me a message through you. Your voice sounded far off but clear and I hope mine was as good. I have not a good telephone voice. On the 26th Oct. I celebrated my 87th birthday and am still in fairly good fettle as I hope you are. You are still a young fellow to me. As I write I can see us all assembled in Lerwick gaol and settling down for 6 days there, all wondering what it was all about. A Naval fiasco indeed!

Once again I repeat my invitation to come to see us when next you travel this way.

Kindest regards to your wife and yourself.

Yours,
J Macmaster

Boars Hill,
Oxford
4th April 58

Dear Mr Manson,

Very many thanks for your letter of 28th March, the copy of the "Postscript" and the newspaper concerning alterations at Lerwick P.O. It seemed to me the alterations were on the right lines. An artist friend once told me that the Lerwick P.O. building was the most artistic P.O. he had ever seen.

I was on holiday and in Bournemouth when a statement was made in the House of Commons anent the Lerwick incident of 1st Nov. 1914. It was far too late and not at all to my mind so I telegraphed to Tait saying that I was not satisfied with it. I merely wanted him to know my view, but I had no wish to interfere in any way with the course to be adopted by the staff. It was up to the staff to do what it considered best in its own interests. When I returned to Lerwick I understood the staff had accepted the Admiralty's donation and I had no feeling at all that you had let me down. It would have pleased me if you had all refused to accept it and I am glad to know – 43 years later – that some were against acceptance. I take off my hat to them. It was a happy idea to present the money to the "Gilbert Bain".

And as we are on the subject of telegrams I want to say this. For several years I sent you a message from Wellingborough on the anniversary and only stopped because I felt it was not fair to my successor at Lerwick.

After I had been at Wellingborough for over 3 years I applied for Kilmarnock which was vacant. I made no reference in my application to the Lerwick incident, but I did say "I have been long enough here", not the most tactful thing to say when seeking promotion. I was still up against H.Q. and not at all inclined towards finesse. Kilmarnock was a poor promotion and if I had been refused it I would have had no doubts about where I stood. I was called to the Secretary's office in London and interviewed by three of the staff. Both sides were on guard and no mention was made of Lerwick. Later I was appointed to Kilmarnock. At K. I was again offered the Admiralty's donation and again refused it in language scarcely polite.

As you may remember I went on from K. to Greenock, Perth and Dundee. Modesty compels me to say that merit alone did not carry me to Dundee. Altho I never made use of the Lerwick affair in seeking promotion, there is no doubt that it helped me a lot. So you see the Lerwick staff of 1914 – or what remains of it – owes me just nothing at all.

I hope that you are now in good fettle and that Mrs Manson and the family are all flourishing.

Kindest regards,

J Macmaster